SHAKEDOWN

SHAKE

Ezra Levant

DOMИ

How Our Government Is Undermining Democracy in the Name of Human Rights

Foreword by Mark Steyn

McClelland & Stewart

Library and Archives Canada Cataloguing in Publication

Levant, Ezra, 1972-
Shakedown : how our government is undermining democracy in the name of human rights / Ezra Levant.

ISBN 978-0-7710-4618-6

1. Civil rights – Canada. 2. Human rights – Canada. I. Title.

JC599.C3'39 2009 323.0971 C2008-904966-7

We acknowledge the financial support of the Government of Canada through the Book Publishing Industry Development Program and that of the Government of Ontario through the Ontario Media Development Corporation's Ontario Book Initiative. We further acknowledge the support of the Canada Council for the Arts and the Ontario Arts Council for our publishing program.

Typeset in Electra by M&S, Toronto
Printed and bound in Canada

McClelland & Stewart Ltd.
75 Sherbourne Street
Toronto, Ontario
M5A 2P9
www.mcclelland.com

1 2 3 4 5 13 12 11 10 09

To my parents for their example,
to my wife for her support,
and to my daughter for her future

CONTENTS

FOREWORD

If you want to know what this book's about, the easiest place to start is with one brief soundbite from Ezra Levant's interrogation by the Alberta "Human Rights" Commission. Ezra had chosen to publish the "Danish cartoons" – the controversial representations of the Prophet Mohammed – in his magazine *The Western Standard*, and as a result had found himself summoned before Shirlene McGovern, a "human rights agent" for the Government of Alberta. And, at one point in her inquisition, after listening to Ezra's musings on the outrageousness of what was happening, Agent McGovern looked blandly across the table and shrugged:

> *"You're entitled to your opinions, that's for sure."*

If only. Clichés are the reflex mechanisms of speech – "Yeah, sure, it's a free country. Everyone's entitled to his opinion, right?" And we get so careless with them that we don't even notice when they become obsolete.

But in Canada you are no longer entitled to your opinion. That cliché is no longer operative. You are only entitled to your opinion if Agent McGovern and her colleagues say you are – "for sure." Canadians do not enjoy the right to free speech. They enjoy instead the right to government-regulated, government-licensed, government-monitored, government-approved speech – which is not the same thing at all. Ezra Levant was of the opinion that he should publish the Danish cartoons. That opinion brought down upon him the full force of the Government of Alberta. I wrote an international bestseller called *America Alone*, a Number One book in Canada, excerpted in the country's oldest and biggest-selling magazine *Maclean's*. The opinions expressed in my book and that magazine excerpt were put on trial for a week in a Vancouver courthouse.

This is not North Korea or Sudan, Ceausescu's Romania or Saddam's Iraq. If it were, what's going on would be easier to spot. So if, like hundreds of thousands of viewers around the world, you go to YouTube and look at the videos of Ezra Levant's interrogation, you will find not a jackbooted thug prowling a torture chamber but a dull bureaucrat asking soft-spoken questions in a boring office. Nevertheless, she is engaged in a totalitarian act.

"You're entitled to your opinions, that's for sure."

No, sorry. If he were, he wouldn't be there. If I'd been entitled to my opinions, I wouldn't have been at the British Columbia "Human Rights" Tribunal. In the Canada of the 21st century, it's the job of Shirlene McGovern and her fellow government "human rights agents" from coast to coast to determine whether you are entitled to your opinions.

That is an abomination to a free society. And that's what this book is about.

Let's take it as read that Ezra Levant and I are, as our critics claim, "offensive." That's the point. It's offensive speech that requires legal protection. If you don't believe in freedom of speech for offensive speech, you don't believe in freedom of speech at all. Anyone can be in favour of Barney the Dinosaur singing "Sharing Is Caring." But any original thinking on almost any issue is likely to be controversial – and offensive to someone, whether you're writing about Islam, abortion, American foreign policy, climate change, or anything else. That's what makes free societies the most dynamic on the planet: they're great big jostling marketplaces of ideas. Ezra and I have a higher opinion of Canadians than Agent McGovern and her fellow thought police do. They think you're wee sensitive delicate creatures who need to be protected by the state from anything that might discombobulate you. We think that, as citizens of one of the oldest settled constitutional democracies on the planet, you're perfectly capable of deciding for yourself what you want to read. You don't need your opinions monitored by government enforcers, some of whom are incompetent, others of whom are corrupt, and none of whom should have the powers they have.

Ezra is an unlikely hero but he is a genuine one. To be sure, as his detractors like to say, he's also a blowhard, a loudmouth, a self-promoter, a "controversy entrepreneur," etc. I speak as one myself. It takes one to know one. If he weren't a blowhard, loudmouth, whatever, his heroism would have been far less effective. Instead, in the space of 12 months, he did more than anyone to transform the reputation of Canada's "human rights" commissions. In November 2007, insofar as anyone was even aware of them, the smiley-face Orwellian name conjured mostly sappy self-flattering delusions about this country's commitment to social progress. A year later, at the policy convention of Canada's governing party, over 99 per cent of delegates voted to abolish the Section 13 "hate speech" provision of the Human Rights Code, and a respected Liberal Member of Parliament filed a motion calling for an inquiry into the conduct of the federal "human rights" commission. And, in implicit acknowledgement of the worst year of publicity in its history, at the end of November 2008, the Canadian "Human Rights" Commission's own report into free speech issues also called for the abolition of Section 13. The decline in reputation of Canada's "human rights" racket in those 12 months was driven principally by the energy and passion Ezra Levant brought to the cause.

The word Ezra used to describe his strategy is "denormalization." Before he and I had the misfortune to attract the attention of our tormentors at the Canadian "Human Rights" Commission, the Alberta "Human Rights" Commission, the Ontario "Human Rights" Commission and the British Columbia "Human Rights" Tribunal, these agencies were merely another unremarkable branch of the Dominion's swollen bureaucracy, headed by Queen's Counsels, officers of the Order of Canada, former mayors of great cities, holders of the Queen's Jubilee Medal, and other paragons of the establishment. Thanks to Ezra's sustained campaign of "denormalization," more and more Canadians now understand that these beribboned eminences preside over an ugly thuggish machine that is incompatible with a free society. In June of 2008, I sat in a courthouse in Vancouver and listened to a week's worth of "expert witnesses" discuss my writing, my jokes, my authorial "tone," and other weighty matters that in civilized jurisdictions would be of concern only to obscure literary critics but which in Canada now get you dragged up before a panel of pseudo-judges. The courthouse looked like any other in the nation: The bar, the witness box, the Royal Coat of Arms on the wall to symbolize the ancient legal inheritance to which this trio of judges claimed title. Yet they should really have hung the arms upside down, with the crown pointing to the floor: The British Columbia "Human Rights" Tribunal inverts every principle of Common Law; it discards real human rights – the right to a fair trial, the right to due process, the right to the presumption of innocence – and supplants them with a set of ersatz "human rights," notably the human right not to be offended, not by no-one, nowhere, no how. That is, if one belongs to certain approved victim groups.

Before they made the strategic miscalculation of going after Ezra's *Western Standard* and then me and *Maclean's*, Canada's "human rights" racket had spent the last 30 years picking on nobodies – minor targets too poor or peripheral to fight back. If you were unlucky enough to attract their attention, you were guilty: in the entire history of the Canadian "Human Rights" Commission, not a single defendant charged with a federal Section 13 "hate speech" crime has ever been acquitted. The sole exception was the "Canadian Nazi Party," which got off scot-free on the quaint technicality that it did not, in fact, exist. (The fact that the CHRC was reduced to prosecuting entirely fictional entities tells you a lot about how necessary Section 13 is to the Queen's peace.)

Alas, if you do have the misfortune to enjoy corporeal existence, your odds of beating the rap are a lot grimmer. Section 13 has a 100 per cent conviction rate that even the justice systems of Kim Jong Il and the Burmese junta might find a tad embarrassing. But not the CHRC. No wonder the apparatchiks seemed to think it entirely natural to extend their reach to mainstream news magazines, and were so taken aback when Ezra and I decided to fight back.

As I said, Ezra is famously noisy, and can sometimes seem like one of those shower units where the merest nudge of the dial sends it straight up to scalding. When he and I began pushing back against the thought police, the naysayers tutted that Canadians weren't going to put up with a couple of self-inflating gasbags going nuclear on "their" beloved human rights commissions. And, for a while, I worried that they might be right. When news of the Canadian Islamic Congress' three suits against *Maclean's* broke at the end of 2007, the magazine received a lot of letters from readers insisting that yes, *of course*, everyone was in favour of freedom of speech, but it was a question of where you draw the line, how you strike a balance, etc. Drawing the line, striking a balance: these are concepts designed to appeal to Canadians' sense of their own moderation. Judging from the initial response, I had the vague feeling we might end up holding the big capacity-only free speech rally in my Honda Civic. For a while, there was more interest abroad than at home, with *The New York Post, The Australian, The Economist* and the BBC taking up the story, while *The Toronto Star* et al stayed silent.

But Ezra was more confident. He understood that, like the undead feasting on human flesh in the dead of night but unable to bear a shaft of sunlight, Canada's "human rights" racket could not withstand the glare of publicity. In a free society, justice must not only be done, but must be seen to be done. And when you see what's being done at the Canadian "Human

Rights" Commission and its provincial siblings it's no surprise that no one other than those benefiting from the racket is prepared to defend it. This book is a portrait of an insane system by a man who has been on the receiving end of it.

As for the case that set Ezra Levant on his great crusade, it's true that very few parts of the western world emerged with credit from the "Danish cartoons" crisis. In France, the sole editor to republish them was fired by his boss. In America, CNN showed the cartoons on TV, but with the Prophet's face all blurry and pixilated – as if the cartoon Mohammed had entered the witness protection program. In Britain, the Foreign Secretary made a pitiful statement of groveling appeasement. And the European Union's Commissioner for Justice and Security proposed a "media code" that would encourage, ah, "prudence" in the way the press covers, ahem, certain touchy subjects.

But only in Canada did the commissars of the state haul a publisher in for interrogation for the alleged "crime" of reprinting the cartoons.

That act shames this country. Ezra Levant has borne his ordeal with great good humor, and has used it to open Canadians' eyes to the abuses of justice committed in the name of pseudo-"human rights" that have less and less to do with the genuine article. He is a true Canadian hero. Read this book, and demand your politicians act upon it.

Mark Steyn

INTRODUCTION

On January 11, 2008, I was summoned to a ninety-minute government interrogation. My crime? As the publisher of *Western Standard* magazine, I had reprinted Danish cartoons depicting the Muslim prophet Mohammed to illustrate a news story. I was charged with the offence of "discrimination" and made to appear before Alberta's Human Rights and Citizenship Commission (AHRCC) for questioning. As crazy as it sounds, I became the only person in the world to face legal sanction for printing those cartoons.

"In an investigation interview," my interrogator, Shirlene McGovern, said, "I always ask people [their intent] . . . what was the intent and purpose of your article with the cartoon illustrations?" That one sentence summed up the commission's illiberal nature. The idea that the government could haul in a publisher and force him to answer questions about his political beliefs didn't seem extraordinary to this woman. Apparently, it was all in a day's work.

And what *was* my intent and purpose? I've been asked that question a hundred times since I published the cartoons, and I always answer the same way: The images – and the reaction they caused – were newsworthy. As a magazine publisher, I am in the news business. My colleagues and I wanted to show our readers what the fuss was about. But when a government officer demanded to know why I'd dared publish the cartoons, that matter-of-fact answer just didn't seem appropriate.

"We published those cartoons for the intention and purpose of exercising our inalienable rights," I declared, my political passions getting the better of my good manners, "to publish whatever the hell we want, no matter what the hell you think."

I recorded the interrogation, and when it was over, I went straight home to upload the footage to YouTube, the Internet video-sharing site. I was proud that I'd stood up for free speech, and I wanted some of my friends and supporters to hear what I'd said.

The videos spread like wildfire. Over the next two days, more than one hundred thousand people watched them – making my interview the fifth most watched video clip on the entire Internet that weekend. No one had ever seen a government bureaucrat grill a journalist about his private thoughts – at least not in a free country such as Canada.

In all, more than six hundred thousand people have watched my January 11 investigation interview. My battle with Canada's human rights commissions – which has since been joined by Mark Steyn, *Maclean's* magazine, and legions of bloggers – has grown bigger than I could ever have imagined.

As a result of my experience, I began investigating other cases in which innocent people have had their freedoms compromised by bureaucrats presuming to protect Canadians' human rights. What I learned shocked me.

Like most Canadians, I had previously associated the term *human rights* with the noble goal of eliminating real discrimination against blacks, Jews, Muslims, gays, women, and other groups that historically have been targeted by bigotry. Yet with little political fanfare or media scrutiny, human rights commissions have shifted their mission in recent years. As real discrimination has waned in our increasingly tolerant society, they have shifted into the field of what George Orwell called "thoughtcrime."

Human rights commissions now monitor political opinions, fine people for expressing politically incorrect viewpoints, censor websites, and even ban people, permanently, from saying certain things. I've also seen how empire building government bureaucrats actively seek out complaints – even absurd complaints that have nothing at all to do with real human rights – to keep a caseload churning through their grievance industry.

It's not just politically incorrect ideas that are under attack. It could be almost anything. I was stunned to discover that Canada's human rights commissions ruled that a McDonald's restaurant in Vancouver had to accommodate an employee who couldn't wash her hands often enough at work. I learned about a Calgary hairstylist who filed a human rights complaint because the girls at salon school called him a "loser." The commission actually had a trial about it. In another case that seemed stranger than fiction, an emotionally unstable transsexual fought for – and won – the right to counsel female rape victims at a women's shelter, despite the anguished pleas of the rape victims themselves not to let him in.

The more I dug, the more I discovered that my interrogation at the hands of the government wasn't unusual. Every day, Canadians from coast to coast are trapped in these *Alice in Wonderland* commissions, where bizarre new human rights are made up on the spot, and where regular legal procedures don't apply. Sometimes, it feels like Saudi justice; sometimes, it smacks of the old Soviet Union; sometimes, it sounds like a *Saturday Night Live* sketch. Rarely does it feel Canadian.

This book is the product of my ordeal and the research it inspired. I want to write the story of how the concept of human rights was turned on its head. I want to warn Canadians about the travesty of justice playing out in commissions across the country. And finally, I want to lead a fight to take back our real civil rights.

Chapter 1

A BEAUTIFUL IDEA – THAT FAILED

If you had to come up with the most appealing name possible for a government bureaucracy, Human Rights Commission would be a top contender. Everyone's in favour of human rights, and if there is a commission that's working to promote them, that's a good thing, right? In an age when many Canadians are quick to associate terms such as *taxes* or *red tape* with government, it's nice to have a bureaucracy with *rights* as its middle name.

When they were created a generation ago, Canada's human rights commissions were inspired by a narrowly defined goal: to offer victims of true discrimination a quick, low-cost means to fight back against bigoted landlords, employers, and storeowners.

A creature of the civil rights era and its aftermath, human rights commissions (HRCs) were supposed to be an equalizer to help the poor and powerless stand up to the rich and powerful. In both the federal and provincial varieties, HRCs were going to take the best from the court system and social work agencies and combine them in an informal, quasi-judicial structure that could move quickly to assist people in dire need – for example, someone kicked out of an apartment in the middle of winter because he is Aboriginal, or someone fired from a job because she is black.

The Canadian Human Rights Act (CHRA), the law that provides the legislative mandate to the biggest and most powerful HRC in the country, the federal government's Canadian Human Rights Commission (CHRC), lays this vision out in grand terms.

> The purpose of this Act is to extend the laws in Canada to give effect . . . to the principle that all individuals should have an opportunity equal with other individuals to make for themselves the lives that they are able and wish to have and to have their needs accommodated, consistent with their duties and obligations as members of society, without being hindered in or prevented from doing so by discriminatory practices based on race, national or ethnic origin, colour, religion, age, sex, sexual orientation, marital status, family status, disability or conviction for an offence for which a pardon has been granted.

Who could object to *that?*

Unlike in regular courts, victims wouldn't have to spend money hiring lawyers – the commissions themselves would investigate problems and put a government lawyer on the file, for free. Trials would be relaxed – not bogged down with all the rules of regular courts that lawyers love but nobody else understands.

HRCs would try hard to settle cases amicably, through mediation – getting a win-win solution if possible – and build bridges of understanding among citizens. In those rare cases where some bigoted bully just wouldn't see the error of his ways, there would be a tribunal – a quasi-court where adjudicators, usually lawyers with a background in human rights campaigns, could issue orders to set things right. It would be a people's court for the kind of people who used to fall through the cracks.

Human rights commissions were a beautiful idea – that failed.

Forty years ago, when Canada's first HRCs were being created, this country was far less multicultural than it is now, and prejudice was commonplace. But powerful social forces were ushering in a welcome change in attitude. The U.S. civil rights movement was on the march, and change was in the air around the world, from the newly independent countries in the Third World to the student protests in Europe to the dissident folk songs of Bob Dylan. The protection of minorities was an important project whose time had come.

That project succeeded in ways that activists of yesteryear would have found unimaginable. As I write these words in November 2008, Barack Obama has just been elected President of the United States. In the 1960s, the idea that Canada could have a female prime minister, a Chinese and then a black Governor General, and openly gay cabinet ministers – and that a majority of the citizens in Canada's biggest city would be minorities – would have seemed like a vision from the twenty-second century. Sometimes we forget how much things have changed since the 1960s, a time when, for example, Aboriginal peoples didn't even have full voting rights. We've come a long way.

The Canada of the twenty-first century is much more diverse and more tolerant. Bob Dylan is a senior citizen now. He doesn't fight against the system, he *is* the system – shilling for everyone from Cadillac to Victoria's Secret. And good for him. That's what happens when the battles are won: The warriors can go home and enjoy themselves.

Women went from being anomalies at universities to making up 50 per cent of Canada's law students and 60 per cent of Canada's medical school enrollees. Jews flooded into once-restricted country clubs. Blacks and Asians took their rightful place in Parliament and provincial legislatures.

The battle for equality just isn't as urgent any more in a country where a Sikh has been premier of British Columbia, and a woman is the chief justice of the Supreme Court. In the face of all this, Canada's HRCs could have declared the war won and done what Bob Dylan did – do a victory lap and enjoy retirement.

But they didn't. By the time the battle against bigotry was being decisively won in the late 1980s and 1990s, the human rights industry spawned by Canada's HRCs had become too big to fold up and throw in the recycling bin. And so new, previously unknown brands of discrimination had to be found for yesterday's anti-racists and their newly recruited colleagues.

That's where things went off the rails: these once-honourable institutions aimed at correcting historic injustices slid into farce. More and more of the complaints that came their way were from crackpot narcissists, angry loners, and professional grievance collectors. Their disputes had nothing to do with human rights as we know the term. But in the absence of legitimate human rights cases, the HRCs took on their causes – with disastrous and sometimes Kafkaesque results. Ironically, an institution devoted to human rights has now become the biggest threat to our core liberties – most notably, freedom of speech.

HRCs began adjudicating garden-variety interpersonal disputes that had only the flimsiest of human rights pretexts. Over the years, HRCs have become a sort of parallel legal system, competing with real courts for cases, while lacking all of their institutional expertise and procedural safeguards.

Alan Borovoy, the seventy-six-year-old general counsel of the Canadian Civil Liberties Association and an Officer of the Order of Canada, was one of the 1960s activists who helped draft the laws that created Canada's first HRCs. As I will discuss in more detail later in this book, he's now become disgusted by the manner in which they've been co-opted by radicals.

Were there any warning signs that Canada's HRCs would stray so far from their original mandate? George Jonas, now a *National Post* columnist, who came to Canada in the wake of the Soviet crackdown on Hungary in 1956, was one of the few skeptical voices when Canada's HRCs took flight. Having fled communism, Jonas knew a thing or two about the natural tendency of government to encroach on every sphere of human activity – often at the expense of individual rights. But he was simply out of synch with the spirit of the times in Canada. No one listened to him. We now wish we had.

When the *Western Standard* magazine was hauled before Alberta's Human Rights and Citizenship Commission for publishing Danish cartoons of the prophet Mohammed, Borovoy said, "We never imagined that [HRCs] might ultimately be used against freedom of speech."

Jonas, an old debating partner of Borovoy, shot back with an I-told-you-so column in the *Post* and recited some of the traditional reasons he's always opposed government intervention in this field. "Human rights laws and tribunals are based on the notion that being hired, promoted, serviced and esteemed is a human right," he wrote. "It isn't. Being hired, promoted, serviced and esteemed is a human ambition. It's a justifiable ambition, but still just an ambition. . . . There are attractive ambitions and ugly rights, but the ugliest right still trumps the prettiest ambition."

But Jonas welcomed his old rival's conversion: "Some argue that lapsed liberals who kept quiet while the state's commissars were targeting marginal journalists in fringe periodicals have zero moral authority to speak when they go after major commentators in mainstream magazines. Nonsense. Relapsed liberals are welcome to speak."

Borovoy and Jonas still trade friendly barbs back and forth in the newspapers these days. But there's really little disagreement between them now – they both think the HRCs have gone too far. Jonas says Borovoy should have known better; Borovoy says he didn't see it coming. But today, both men want to pull the plug.

What would happen if the plug *were* pulled on the country's HRCs?

The fact is, the human rights situation for Canadians wouldn't change much. Most cases that fill the dockets at HRCs are already covered by other courts or quasi-judicial tribunals. In Alberta, for example, the greatest number of human rights complaints is from young white men. The most common scenario involves a young worker injured on a construction job site who wants more compensation than he was contractually permitted under his union agreement, insurance policy, or the province's workers' compensation board.

HRCs were set up to help minorities who were being picked on, not construction workers who discovered a loophole to make a quick $5,000. But bizarre as it may be, this phenomenon is also encouraging, in its way: if there weren't so little real discrimination out there, this sort of nonsense litigation wouldn't be dominating our HRCs.

Alberta provides a great case study of HRCs. The province is booming, not just economically but demographically. Hundreds of thousands of newcomers have streamed in over the past few years from across Canada and outside the country. Despite the fact that Alberta now has a more diverse population than ever before, complaints to the Alberta Human Rights and Citizenship Commission have actually *fallen* in recent years. Its latest annual report revealed that the total number of complaints received plummeted 15 per cent in a single year, from 778 to 659 – and most of those complaints evaporated away before the first hearing.

In the private sector, a company that experienced a 15 per cent drop in customers in a growing market would either have to lay off staff or go out of business. But it's tough to put human rights commissions out of business, since they get their money from the government no matter how obsolete their "product" has become.

The AHRCC takes more time than ever to achieve a result. According to the AHRCC's own statistics, the average time it takes the agency to resolve a complaint has increased by a month, from 382 days to 410 – this from a people's court that originally was supposed to be a speedy and informal alternative to real courts. What good is a fourteen-month delay to someone who's been kicked out of an apartment in the middle of winter, or fired from a job with just a month's rent in the bank?

There's something a little dishonest about a government agency that has 15 per cent less work to do, takes 7 per cent more time to do it, and still gets the same cheque each year from the government. The AHRCC knows this, so it's come up with a clever plan to drum up new business. Like private companies who want more customers, the HRC has started a marketing campaign, trying to convince Albertans to complain more about one another.

Like any savvy – or desperate – marketer, the human rights commission targeted the group of Albertans it thought would be most easily convinced to use their services. It made a deal with the province's Ministry of Advanced Education to publish sixty thousand easy-to-read booklets encouraging people to file complaints, and to have the ministry distribute those booklets to new immigrants who were studying English as a Second Language. The booklet was styled as a textbook to help these newcomers learn English. No *Dick and Jane* for those new Albertans. They'd be learning how to complain as they learned their ABC's.

The booklet takes the form of a series of stories that new immigrants are expected to relate to and, like any good ESL book, they are accompanied by helpful pictures to illustrate the words. One of the stories in the pamphlet is about "Angela," a middle-aged black woman with dreadlocks, shown sitting alone in a restaurant. The full text that accompanies the image is this: "I was in a restaurant one day. I was the only black customer. The server didn't come to my table for a long time. When she came to my table, she wasn't very polite to me. I think the server discriminated against me because of my colour."

That's it: a slow waitress. The fictitious waitress didn't say anything rude and certainly nothing racist. She didn't refuse to serve "Angela." She was just a little slow – kind of like the AHRCC itself. The message to those sixty thousand new immigrants is clear: no matter how trivial or speculative your problem, you should always assume the culprit is racism – and you should always run to the human rights commission to fix it.

Of course, in a booming economy such as Alberta's, it's tough for restaurateurs (and anyone else) to recruit good service staff. In a province where 7-Eleven convenience stores offer huge cash bonuses for clerks who stay on for three months and fast-food restaurants pay as much as $15 an hour, occasionally getting rude service is a fact of life. It's the result of the tight labour market. It's not racism.

In any case, there are a lot of things that normal people would do in a situation such as "Angela's." They could leave a smaller tip, complain to the manager – or to the waitress herself. They could even do what the rest of us do: grumble to ourselves and to our friends, and vow never to return to the restaurant again. But none of those remedies gin up work for bureaucrats who get paid to handle racism. And so they promote a world view in which self-reliance has been extinguished.

There are plenty of other absurd examples in that HRC marketing document – including a confusing example about whether office jokes are funny, unfunny, or a violation of human rights. (Answer: If they're not funny, they're discrimination.) But the craziest example has to be the HRC's lesson about a student named "Kau." The brochure shows a photograph of a young man of Asian descent with unkempt hair, wearing a casual hoodie sweater at a job interview in a boardroom. It was no surprise to me he didn't get the job; he's dressed like a skateboarding high-schooler. But according to "Kau's story," it was a case of racism – because the interviewer asked him about his accent, and whether he was from China. According to the brochure, that's discrimination on the basis of country of origin – a type of racism that "Kau" should take up with the AHRCC.

Stop for a moment to think about the faulty internal logic at play here. Would a racist employer even grant an interview to someone with an obviously non-anglo, non-French name such as "Kau"? And if she didn't know Kau was Asian in the first place, she'd figure it out pretty quickly when he showed up – from his facial features, or accent, or resumé, or all three – wouldn't she?

But even putting aside the sheer dumbness of the depicted scenario, it's worth asking why new Albertans are being conditioned to expect the worst from their fellow human beings. In thirty years of AHRCC jurisprudence, there hasn't been a single case of a Chinese would-be employee who was discriminated against on the basis of "national origin." Today in Alberta, the job market is so tight, employers are literally flying in foreign workers, especially for the oil patch. Being racist – as Jonas points out – is a costly prejudice in a tight economy.

Why do AHRCC staff feel compelled to drum up business by teaching eager new immigrants that the Canadian way is to gripe to the government about any slight, real or imagined? Do they think it's *good* for national morale when taxpayer-funded agencies portray Canada as a country full of racists and teach newcomers that bigotry lurks in every coffee shop? That may describe the way of life in some of the countries the new immigrants came from, but it doesn't describe their adopted homeland.

Of course, Canadians should have somewhere to go if their path in life is blockaded by bigotry. But HRCs are redundant because they duplicate the roles of other institutions.

Take employment law. It states that firing someone solely for being black or gay or Jewish is called firing "without cause." The courts won't require the employer to rehire the employee, but they will order the employer to pay the employee a severance package, and if the employee was fired in an abusive manner, the amount is increased substantially. That has been the law long before human rights commissions were invented.

The principles of landlord and tenant law are also well established in the Western legal tradition. It tends to be extremely tenant-friendly in most Canadian jurisdictions, so that it is difficult to evict tenants even for just cause. Many cities have volunteer legal services to help tenants fight evictions or even rent increases. Those predate human rights commissions, and they can usually help tenants the same day, not 410 days later.

Real courts are still a hassle for the downtrodden – as they are for everyone else. Let's face it, litigation is never fun. But over the past forty years, the legal profession has initiated steps to help poor people who can't afford lawyers. Law societies tell lawyers that part of their professional responsibility is to do some pro bono work for poor clients, and many lawyers take that responsibility seriously. And every law school in the country has clubs whose law student members volunteer one night a week in a downtown legal clinic, helping drop-ins with every conceivable legal problem, from minor criminal matters to contract disputes. Despite their low budgets, these volunteer sector endeavours are often more effective.

When 1960s-vintage activists such as Borovoy advocated the creation of HRCs, they envisioned them as agencies that would not only resolve specific grievances, but also take a leading role in advocating on behalf of minorities. That vision has come to pass: Many HRC judgments read like press releases for left-wing NGOs.

But even if all the nation's HRCs shuttered their doors tomorrow, Canada would hardly be short of advocates for tolerance.

Canada in the twenty-first century is chock full of civil rights lobby groups, many of which are far more effective at building racial and religious harmony than Canada's HRCs. Every possible faction, ethnic group, and political perspective has its own group these days, many with multimillion-dollar budgets. And Canada's female, gay, Muslim, Chinese, Jewish, black, and disabled politicians hardly need to be informed by HRCs – or anyone else – about what minorities think about this or that issue.

Some might argue that it never hurts to add more voices to the mix. But I'm not so sure. When the government gets into the civil rights business, it sends the message that policing our social mores is a job for Big Brother. That message, in turn, crowds out individuals and private groups that would otherwise handle the task. If there's no need to write letters to the editor, call in to talk-radio shows, join political campaigns, and go to public town halls – because a government agency is already supposedly taking care of it all for us – we lose track of our responsibilities, as citizens, to build a proper civil society through our own actions. And there's another problem with government-funded lobby efforts: They're open to political interference, to punish political opponents and go easy on political friends – or, at the very least, to become stacked with patronage appointees.

Since I began my campaign against HRCs, some of my opponents within the human rights industry have attempted to smear me as an enemy of human rights. I am no such thing. A respect for human rights has become one of Canada's great hallmarks. What I oppose are not human rights themselves but the hijacking of these rights by dysfunctional, self-interested government agencies that lost track of what the term means a long time ago.

I hope that by the time you've finished reading this book, you'll agree with me.

Chapter 2

WHERE DID WE GO WRONG?

Human rights commissions aren't real courts, though they often dress themselves up in judicial trappings. Most don't even have formal rules of procedure.

The procedural rules followed by Canadian courts – criminal courts in particular – have developed over centuries, stretching back all the way to Magna Carta, the great charter forced on England's King John in 1215 by angry noblemen upset with his abusive practices. The Magna Carta imposed limits on the King's power. He was no longer allowed to seize land or people without just cause or to arbitrarily use the law to fill his coffers and impoverish his enemies. The charter strengthened the right to habeas corpus – a Latin phrase we still use today to describe the right of prisoners to have a hearing to determine whether their detention is valid. It stated that fines and other punishments should be proportionate to the offence. And it guaranteed speedy trials.

Those basic rights, established in England almost eight hundred years ago, are the foundations of our Canadian court system today. Even Canadians who don't know the details of our judicial processes have developed an instinct for what's fair and what's not. That instinct reflects what law school professors like to call "natural justice." It feels natural because, after eight hundred years, it's been woven into every aspect of our culture.

The main reason that today's human rights commissions feel so un-Canadian is that their operations violate the most basic principles of natural justice. As soon as a human rights complaint is filed, the deck is stacked against the accused. For most of Canada's HRCs, taxpayers foot the bill so that government-paid bureaucrats can investigate complaints and government-paid lawyers can prosecute them. The targets of those complaints, on the other hand, don't get any government help. Many are too poor to hire lawyers and private investigators, so they must fend for themselves against an army of public paper-pushers. (A study of the cases in which the Canadian Human Rights Commission investigated allegations of hate speech, for example, found that 91 per cent of the government's targets were too poor to afford lawyers and appeared either on their own or with representation by a non-lawyer volunteer.) In other words, it's a turkey shoot for the government, with poor, intimidated targets fighting against the unlimited resources of the state.

Contrast this with the procedures used in Canadian criminal courts, where defendants who can't afford a lawyer are assigned a lawyer paid for by a provincial legal aid fund or by a charitable group such as the John Howard Society.

There are some important differences between human rights commissioners and judges. A real judge in a real court would feel uncomfortable allowing a trial to proceed against an unrepresented accused criminal. In human rights commissions, by contrast, it's just another way to rack up convictions.

Judges are appointed for life and can only be removed for misconduct. Human rights commissioners are political appointees whose mandate (and paycheque) runs for a short term. They are at the mercy of politicians.

Judges in criminal courts are expected to be neutral. (And if they have any bias, it tends to be in favour of the criminals – since many judges were criminal lawyers before their appointment to the bar.) Even if a judge was previously active in politics or activism, he or she is expected to abandon all of those affiliations when ascending to the bench. The Canadian Judicial Council – the governing body that disciplines judges – is crystal clear on the subject of partisanship. According to their rulebook, "all partisan political activity and association must cease absolutely and unequivocally with the assumption of judicial office."

In contrast, human rights adjudicators often act as partisan advocates for human rights complainants – and sometimes even continue to hold elected political offices and campaign in elections.

In Alberta, Human Rights Commissioner Diane Colley-Urquhart is not only a sitting Calgary alderman, but also a director of both a federal and provincial political party riding association. She's also on the Calgary Police Commission and the city's land use committee. Would Colley-Urquhart's political opponents at City Hall feel they stood a chance if they had to appear before her? How about someone who campaigned against her in an election? If a land developer appeared before her in a human rights trial on Monday, might he plead guilty so that his condo development would get a smoother hearing from her at the city's planning committee on Tuesday? What happens if Colley-Urquhart hears an AHRCC case involving someone who donated money to her alderman campaign? What if both the complainant *and* the target did?

These aren't merely hypothetical risks. In 2008, Colley-Urquhart ruled that a bouncer at Calgary's Tequila Nightclub had improperly denied entry to a Sikh university student who had been waiting in line during a Calgary Stampede event *four years earlier.* The absurdly long delay in hearing the case meant that club owner Harry Dimitriadis couldn't investigate the facts himself. He didn't even know who the bouncer had been that night.

The complainant didn't bother to investigate the facts of the matter either. Though he was angry enough to file a complaint demanding cash, he apparently hadn't been angry enough to ask to speak to a manager that night, or even to get details about the bouncer who'd allegedly treated him shabbily.

For his part, Dimitriadis said the accusations were absurd. He had many regular customers who were Sikh, including several who wore turbans in the club, and he was ready to call them as witnesses. Colley-Urquhart didn't dispute that Dimitriadis ran a multicultural night club, but ruled against the unidentified doorman anyway – ordering Dimitriadis to pay $5,350 plus interest to the student.

Dimitriadis says he'll fight the decision and appeal it to a real court. But I wonder how comfortable he will feel doing this – because Colley-Urquhart isn't just a human rights commissioner and a political operative. She's also the chair of the city's License and Community Standards Appeal Board. If Tequila Nightclub is the subject of a noise complaint or a liquor violation, it is possible that Colley-Urquhart could be his judge again. Is it really good business for him to appeal her punitive human rights order, even though it is clearly legal junk?

An even more disturbing aspect of HRC staffing is the extraordinary prevalence of human rights commissioners who moonlight as radical social activists. These opportunists have figured out a way to use the coercive power of the state to entrench their beloved left-wing social engineering schemes into law – all at taxpayers' expense.

Take the B.C. Human Rights Tribunal (BCHRT). In this capacity, it once commandeered the entire B.C. education ministry, ordering every school district across the province to enact a particular special-needs education program that it thought was necessary. It commanded every school district to follow the BCHRT's particular vision of schooling. Why bother trying to get elected to cabinet when the real policy-making power lies with the human rights commissions?

Some of the BCHRT's nuttiest decisions will be analyzed in detail in later chapters – from ordering a comedian to stand trial because of his attempt at humour, to ordering a community centre to hire a man as a rape crisis counsellor, to presiding over the trial of *Maclean's* magazine for "Islamophobia." The chair of the BCHRT, Heather MacNaughton, is a career activist who cut her teeth in Ontario as then-premier Bob Rae's appointee to that province's Human Rights Commission (OHRC), as well as to its Pay Equity Commission and employment quota commission. I find it difficult to think of a radical social engineering experiment that MacNaughton has not dabbled in. How could anyone in the B.C. government have believed that with this history she would not bring her agenda to the province's human rights bureaucracy?

Or how about Raja Khouri, who was appointed to the OHRC in September 2006? Khouri once served as the president of the Canadian Arab Federation, a group that promotes 9/11 conspiracy theories and that often has been accused of anti-Semitism. Just three months before he was brought on board the OHRC, Khouri wrote a stunning editorial column in the *Globe and Mail*, describing Canada's decision to outlaw the Palestinian terrorist group Hamas as "shameful." (When Hezbollah, another Muslim terrorist group, was banned by Canada in 2002, Khouri had complained too.) Would anyone trust a person with such a clear bias to involve himself in, say, the case of a Jew accused of "Islamophobia"?

Even the human rights commissioners who aren't left-wing activists or political hacks typically lack the sort of legal expertise required to judge their fellow citizens in the name of the state. None of them are judges, and some aren't even lawyers. Colley-Urquhart, for instance, trained as a nurse.

At the Manitoba Human Rights Commission, just to pick a provincial HRC at random, a high school diploma is considered training enough to determine what's legal and what's not, and who has to pay fines and who doesn't. Take Commissioner Joan Hay. Her job title at her day job is community helper at the Ma Mawi Wi Chi Itata Centre, an Aboriginal social service centre in Winnipeg. The official Manitoba HRC biography of fellow commissioner Mzilikazi Ndlovu notes that he grew up in a nature reserve in Zimbabwe, "where entertainment consisted of singing acappella and sliding down a mountain slope on a flat rock," and where "formal education was non-existent." Good for Ndlovu that he managed to earn a political science degree from the University of Winnipeg. But how exactly did he – or any of the other legal amateurs discussed in this book – gain any expertise to make legal decisions that go to the heart of our constitutional freedoms?

The anything-goes amateurism pervading Canada's human rights commissions is readily apparent when it comes time to present evidence. Real courts limit the sort of evidence that can be used against the accused. For instance, hearsay (statements that a witness recalls hearing from someone else) typically isn't allowed except in unusual circumstances, such as in the case of a dying man's last words. But at HRC hearings, the hearsay flies thick and fast. In other words, HRCs allow second-hand gossip to be treated as fact.

Consider what happened, for instance, when *Maclean's* magazine got hauled before the BCHRT for publishing Mark Steyn's October 2006 article "The Future Belongs to Islam," an excerpt from his bestselling book, *America Alone: The End of the World as We Know It.*

The essay was a provocative look at radical Islam – and what Muslim immigration and birth rates would mean for the West. It generated an enormous response, and *Maclean's* published no fewer than twenty-seven letters to the editor in reply, across the entire spectrum of opinion. That's what public debates are supposed to be like.

The grandly named Canadian Islamic Congress (CIC) missed that debate, however. A major discussion about Islam, published on the cover of Canada's most widely read newsmagazine, somehow didn't register with the self-appointed guardians of Islam's sensitivities. When the CIC finally noticed the story, some six months later, they didn't write a letter to the editor. But they certainly made up for lost time. The CIC sent several law students to *Maclean's* headquarters, where they demanded that *Maclean's* give them equal space – including the magazine's cover – for their own rebuttal to the Steyn essay and a list of more than a dozen other articles the CIC felt offended Islam. They also demanded cash. And when they didn't get either, they slapped *Maclean's* with a human rights complaint. Three of them, in fact.

That complaint was brought by Mohamed Elmasry, the radical president of the Canadian Islamic Congress (CIC). But Elmasry (who I will discuss in greater detail later in this book) didn't testify as a witness, even though he claimed to have "suffered" from the allegedly Islamophobic content of Mark Steyn's article. He didn't even show up at the Vancouver trial. Instead, he dispatched a young law student named Khurrum Awan.

Awan wasn't the complainant. He merely had done some legal research for Elmasry. Awan was called by Elmasry's lawyer to give evidence against *Maclean's* on Elmasry's behalf and amazingly, the BCHRT let Awan take the stand. A real judge would have laughed this sort of stunt out of the courtroom. Properly trained judges want to hear from the accuser, not his spokesmodel. And real courts allow the targets of lawsuits to face their accusers. That's a basic element of natural justice.

But Awan wasn't just a surrogate witness for Elmasry. It turns out he was also a surrogate witness giving hearsay evidence regarding what yet another third party felt about *Maclean's* magazine – that third party being one of Awan's fellow law students, who was sitting just a few feet away in the same Vancouver courtroom. And to top it off, an apparent conflict of interest: the commission lawyer who was asking Awan these questions had agreed to hire Awan to his law firm later that year. So Awan was taking questions from his future boss.

Heather MacNaughton and the other tribunal members sat there and let this charade continue for hours. The lawyers from *Maclean's* were jumping up and down with objections, but to no avail. What was the point in having lawyers? There were no laws being followed.

Even in the mother of all HRCs, the Canadian Human Rights Commission, where there is a written list of procedures, the procedures are treated more as suggestions than as rules – at least when applied to the government. Violations of basic due process standards are commonplace. In the high-profile case of alleged white supremacist Marc Lemire, for example, documents forming the CHRC's hate speech case against him weren't disclosed until *after* the trial was over.

In real courts, the police and prosecution have a duty to turn over every scrap of information to the defendant – in the case of criminal charges, that even includes photocopies of police officers' handwritten notes – well before the trial starts. If it later turns out that the police didn't disclose material that could have served to exonerate the accused, the judge typically orders a retrial or outright acquittal.

Lemire kept asking for more documents all the way through his trial – twenty-six days of hearings spread out over a year and a half in 2007 and 2008. Finally, two months after all the witnesses had testified and Lemire had no chance to ask them any more questions, the CHRC disclosed to Lemire hundreds of pages detailing their case against him. But even then they didn't provide full disclosure, unilaterally blacking out whatever information they didn't want Lemire to receive. That was a clear violation of the Canadian Human Rights Tribunal's Rule 6, which requires that the human rights commission "provide a copy of the document[s] to all other parties," and that the CHRC had to continue turning over evidence if the original disclosure was "inaccurate or incomplete." (In Lemire's case, the abuse of Rule 6 was especially flagrant: At trial, the chair of the tribunal demanded to see the CHRC's documents himself, and saw them – but still refused to give them to Lemire.)

Disclosure in the B.C. human rights trial of *Maclean's* magazine was even zanier, if that's possible. The Canadian Islamic Congress gave copies of some of their documents to *Maclean's* the night before the hearing – not weeks before, as they had been ordered to do. At one point in the trial, proceedings had to stop as everyone waited for the CIC's documents to be printed out at a local Kinko's. Then they were rushed to the court – which is when lawyers from *Maclean's* got their first look at them.

Maclean's magazine eventually won its case in the BCHRT. But the fact that it even had to go through a trial after having the identical complaint dismissed by both the federal and Ontario human rights commissions shows the abusiveness of the system. Unlike most targets of the HRCs, the popular magazine had the money to run a five-day show trial, and had it lost, appeal its case to a real court that would apply real constitutional principles, such as freedom of the press. That's likely the very reason why *Maclean's* was acquitted: the human rights mandarins knew that the national media would kick up a huge uproar if an established national media outlet was censored based on the complaints of a few thin-skinned complainers-of-fortune. *Maclean's* wasn't let go because it was "innocent." It was let go because it was too big and powerful for the BCHRT to crush – for now. It took forty-seven pages of legal acrobatics for the BCHRT to try to explain why *Maclean's* should go free, while other B.C. publications that had written similar critical essays had been convicted. It is nothing short of bizarre to read three BCHRT bureaucrats write what is essentially an official government book review – a book review that cost B.C. taxpayers hundreds of thousands of dollars. They "ruled" that Steyn's essay contained "numerous factual, historical and religious inaccuracies about Islam and Muslims," but didn't list a single error. Their official condemnation of the book took the form of disagreeing with Steyn's interpretation of the facts, not with the facts themselves. The province of British Columbia now has an officially correct view of radical Islam – it is not a threat – and all other views are "inaccurate."

Maclean's was officially acquitted, but it is inaccurate to say that it won. The magazine had to pay hundreds of thousands of dollars to defend itself. Unlike real courts, HRCs have no provisions that require unsuccessful complainants to pay the costs incurred by a victorious defendant. And the BCHRT has served them, and every other Canadian magazine, with ominous notice: if *Maclean's* dares to publish "inaccurate" opinions on any subject again, it does so at the risk of being hauled through another half-million-dollar process.

One of the main reasons why Canada isn't as lawsuit-crazy as the United States is the Canadian principle of "loser pays." Anyone who files a lawsuit against someone else in Canada – for anything from breaking a contract to a car accident – knows that if they don't have a good case, they're going to wind up paying not only for their own legal fees but also for a good portion of the other side's fees. The rule acts as a damper on civil lawsuits. It means fewer lawsuits are filed, and fewer still go very far before both sides settle. It adds a healthy whiff of fear to the act of initiating litigation.

That fear is absent where human rights commissions are concerned. Not only do complainants face no downside if they lose – or even if they abandon their complaint after a lengthy process – but they are explicitly protected from being sued for malicious prosecution.

Typical in this regard is Section 10 of Alberta's Human Rights Code, which prohibits vindicated human rights defendants from suing human rights complainants for the costs incurred. No doubt, this sort of anti-"retaliation" provision – which appears in human rights statutes across the country in one form or another – was designed to protect legitimate human rights whistle-blowers. But a provision that may have seemed enlightened forty years ago now mainly serves to protect vexatious complainants from suffering the rightful consequences of their actions. The human rights shield has been turned into a sword.

What happens if someone simply ignores a human rights commission? If they're not real courts, why should anyone even open mail from them, let alone appear before their tribunals? Can an HRC break down your door? The answer is "yes."

Canada's HRCs possess powers that even real police forces don't have. For police to enter your workplace, they need a search warrant, approved by a judge. But many human rights commissions needn't jump through that hoop. Take Newfoundland's HRC, for example. Under Section 22 of that province's human rights code, any HRC officer can "enter a building, factory, workshop or other premises or place in the province a) to inspect, audit and examine books of account, records and documents; or b) to inspect and view a work, material, machinery, an appliance or article found there." That's quite a broad shopping list. And all of it can be done without a search warrant. A human rights busybody only has to decide that you have something he or she wants to see – and presto, instant access.

And the powers of the HRCs aren't limited to inanimate objects – such as your private records, computer hard drive, and chequebook. Those same laws give the HRCs staggering powers over people too. Again, from the Newfoundland law: "The persons occupying or in charge of that [inspected] building, factory, workshop, premises or place shall c) answer all questions concerning those matters put to them; and d) produce for inspection the books of account, records, documents, material, machinery, appliance or article requested."

Answer all questions the government asks, without a warrant? Contrast this with the way legally mandated searches usually work. If police officers came into your office without a search warrant, you'd have the right to invite them to leave – and charge them with trespass if they didn't. And even if they *had* a search warrant, you'd be under no compulsion to act as their personal deputy.

The idea that a person must "answer all questions" put to them is itself a clear violation of our constitutional rights – as anyone who has ever watched an episode of *Law & Order* knows. In the United States, citizens are protected by something called the Fifth Amendment to the Constitution; in Canada, it's Section 11 of our Charter of Rights and Freedoms (not to mention Section 8 of our Charter, which forbids unreasonable search and seizure).

Amazingly, we have set up a system in Canada whereby human rights commissions – staffed by people who have no training in police procedures or any substantive legal knowledge of criminal procedure – have been granted powers that real police don't have except in countries such as Iran.

Canadians in general are vigilant about police abuses – and police chiefs take self-restraint very seriously, employing checks and balances ranging from internal affairs departments to special-complaints panels for citizens upset with the behaviour of individual officers. Yet not a single human rights commission in Canada has an internal affairs department monitoring its staff members' conduct. And there is no place to go to complain about the HRCs themselves. If you have a problem, your only effective recourse is to run to the media (or, in my case, write a book).

But that's not all. At the Canadian Human Rights Commission, the abuse of process goes deeper: trial transcripts reveal that the staff of the CHRC's anti-hate squad, in their bid to entrap alleged hate-mongers, actually have become one of Canada's largest sources of hate speech.

It's hard to believe, but government bureaucrats, paid with tax dollars, who are supposed to be promoting human rights and interracial relations, are spending their time becoming members of neo-Nazi websites and writing bigoted comments on the Internet. Their goal is to goad Canadian citizens into replying with their own hateful comments – which the human rights investigators can then prosecute as human rights abuses.

That would be like a police officer setting out lines of cocaine at a party, snorting a few himself, then inviting other people to do the same – and then arresting them when they take him up on his offer.

CHRC staff have used false codenames – Jadewarr, Axetogrind, Pogue Mahone, and others – to become members of U.S. white supremacist sites such as stormfront.org and Vanguard News Network and join in – and sometimes lead – international discussions, whipping up anti-black, anti-Semitic, and anti-gay sentiment. They encourage racists to organize, and to get out and be "dangerous."

These bizarre tactics are against the law – specifically, Section 13 of the Canadian Human Rights Act, the hate speech law that the CHRC itself is supposed to enforce. But it's been going on for years. Sometimes, there are so many anti-hate bureaucrats online at once, each pretending to be a neo-Nazi, that they bump into each other in the same chat group, both in their Nazi personas, and join the same bigoted conversation.

One day in August 2004, for instance, neo-Nazi members of Stormfront were having a discussion about organizing a white supremacist rally in Vancouver. An Edmonton police officer named Stephen Camp chimed in under his false identity of "Estate." He said the rally should really be in Alberta, but that he "hopes plans in B.C. go well." Soon, another "anti-hate" activist, a former CHRC staffer named Richard Warman, joined in under his false name "Pogue Mahone." "It's good to see the organizing in the West is continuing," he wrote. "Keep it up, brothers!"

There's no telling how many other people on that neo-Nazi website were also in on the game. Given the number of bureaucrats in this country who we pay to monitor hate speech, it's possible that no one on that Stormfront chat was a real neo-Nazi. When the anti-hate activists are a leading source of hate, it's time to get a new moral compass.

Warman, who worked at the CHRC as an anti-hate investigator, is responsible for hundreds of bigoted comments under various aliases. Posting hate apparently became something of a habit: Warman kept up his hobby long after he left the CHRC. Some of his posts were so caustic they could strip paint. He wrote that white police officers "should stand by their race"; that Canadians should create an all-white city where minorities weren't allowed; that the Canadian government's cabinet was full of Jewish "scum"; that gays were "sexual deviants" who were a "cancer," and on and on. The guy is so convincing in his neo-Nazi role that he should be in Hollywood, teaching method acting.

On occasion, CHRC staff would use their alter egos to further their own personal agendas too. Take the case of a teenaged girl named Elizabeth Lampman. Her boyfriend was a bad apple, and she started running with the wrong crowd. She posted some racist comments on a U.S. website. When Warman found out her identity, he hauled her before the CHRC on a hate speech complaint.

Unlike most people charged under Section 13, Lampman didn't fight the charge. She wasn't really a Nazi – she just went along with her boyfriend to fit in with his odious clique. And since they broke up, she had abandoned his politics and started to reconcile with her family. She was just a teenager who wanted to get her life back on the right track.

"That isn't me," she wrote in a private letter to the CHRC. "I was the girl in grade school who befriended the new girl when nobody wanted to play with her because she was Black. I was wrong in following that [neo-Nazi] crowd and am sincerely sorry for anyone I may have hurt or offended through my actions. I am truly ashamed for having strayed so far from the good things I was taught."

She did what the CHRC asked her to do: She renounced her racist views. So the CHRC let her go.

But not Warman. He got his hands on a copy of Lampman's letter and leaked it to a friend, who dutifully put it on the Internet – a confidential, intensely private letter that was sent to the CHRC. Then Warman signed on to a neo-Nazi website using his false name, Axetogrind, and published a link to

Lampman's letter, accompanied by the phrase *with friends like these*. I can only guess that his goal was to "out" Lampman as a traitor to the neo-Nazi movement.

Warman was throwing Lampman to the wolves – even though she had done exactly what the CHRC had asked her to do. The very next neo-Nazi who commented on the website wrote, "Talk about kissing Jew Boots!" If, as the CHRC argues, these neo-Nazi websites really are populated by violent people, then Warman had exposed Lampman to genuine danger, as well as compromising her privacy and violating the promise of privacy the CHRC had given. Warman even published Lampman's name with a flourish of his own bigotry, calling on fellow website Nazis to support Matthew Hale, a white supremacist convicted of plotting to kill a U.S. judge.

During a legal hearing two years later, when Warman's secret identity as Axetogrind was revealed, he was asked about his actions. At first, Warman made the laughable claim that he published her secret letter "to show that individuals were willing to leave the [Nazi] movement and that people should be aware of that." But after a few minutes of cross-examination, he admitted that he hadn't really given the morality of his action any thought.

"You weren't concerned about her security?"

"No," he replied.

"The truth is, Mr. Warman, you didn't care, correct?"

"No," he admitted.

So there you have it: CHRC staff and CHRC alumni having their own neo-Nazi ball on the Internet, posting hateful messages that are in direct violation of the very law they are meant to uphold. They do it with the knowledge and consent of CHRC management, often during work hours, using CHRC computers or on their own, to conduct obscure vendettas against private citizens.

Does Parliament know what our so-called anti-hate bureaucrats are up to? Do voters? If they did, would they continue to fork over $25 million a year to the CHRC?

In August 2006, a human rights complaint was actually filed against Warman for breaking the CHRC's own rules. A CHRC investigator wrote that Warman "did re-post some material that could be found to be a violation of Section 13 of the CHRA," and that his "actions do amount to communicating hate messages." But the complaint – which was filed by someone the CHRC was investigating – was dropped in short order.

And yet, it's not the first time that a government agency has propped up hate. In the 1980s and 1990s, Canada's spy agency, the Canadian Security Intelligence Service (CSIS), planted an operative named Grant Bristow in the middle of the neo-Nazi movement. Bristow was ostensibly sent in to keep an eye on potentially violent members. But he didn't just passively act as CSIS's eyes and ears; he actively helped build the Heritage Front into Canada's largest neo-Nazi group. Bristow – and CSIS – created the biggest racist gang in the country, a project that only ended when Bristow's double identity was about to be discovered.

Your tax dollars at work.

At least Bristow was an agent for a real spy organization, with a real oversight committee, called The Security Intelligence Review Committee (SIRC). But even with all of the checks and balances imposed by SIRC, he was still out of control, veering off mission, getting a little too deep into his dual life as a neo-Nazi.

CSIS and Bristow started to use the Heritage Front as a political weapon, trying to take over the then-nascent Reform Party and turn it into a white power organization – a "spy mission" that just happened to benefit the two leading parties at the time, the Progressive Conservatives and the Liberals, who just happened to have appointed the CSIS chief and the members of the SIRC oversight committee. The Reform Party caught that attempted infiltration and stopped it, but not without some embarrassing media coverage.

Every generation witnesses some variation on this game: a government agency helps to build up isolated hate-mongers into national menaces and then points to its own handiwork as proof that more government power and tax money is necessary to save us.

In the 1960s, the Canadian Jewish Congress (CJC) paid John Garrity, a small-time mercenary, to build up the fledgling Canadian Nazi Party. As with the CHRC today and Bristow twenty years ago, Garrity's mission was justified as an attempt to learn more about neo-Nazism. Garrity – and the CJC's money – built the Canadian Nazi Party into a media sensation. There's something wrong with an anti-hate industry that is so devoid of targets that its leaders have to bankroll and promote their enemies just to justify their own existence.

All these schemes and fronts and double agents just aren't the Canadian way – it feels more like the petty cloak-and-dagger schemes of a small-time police state such as Syria or the Palestinian Authority, with different spy agencies spying on each other, each sowing paranoia and becoming paranoid in turn.

The CHRC knows its antics wouldn't survive public scrutiny, and so it often tries to suppress public access to its inner working. Besides ignoring its own disclosure requirements, it routinely refuses to comply with Access to Information requests despite a legal obligation to do so. And when the CHRC brings cases to trial at the Canadian Human Rights Tribunal (CHRT), the commission often demands – and gets – an order to keep the trial secret. In the hate speech trial of Marc Lemire, the CHRC actually applied for an order to exclude Lemire himself from the courtroom when the CHRC brought its evidence. Even Stalin's show trials allowed their political criminals to be in the room when they were being set up.

For decades, the CHRC preferred to operate in the shadows, and nobody in the mainstream media or Parliament seemed to care much. The CHRC may have broken every rule in the book, but since its agents were mainly going after the poor and powerless – who were often distastefully rude, and sometimes even bigoted racists – no one in Ottawa or the media seemed to care.

That changed when the CHRC and the other HRCs started going after more mainstream political opponents – including the media itself. Suddenly, a lot of rocks were being turned over.

At a Canadian Human Rights Tribunal hearing on March 25, 2008, accused hatemonger Marc Lemire directly challenged the CHRC's habit of going online using false neo-Nazi identities. His argument was that any bigoted comments on his own website were in fact written by the CHRC to set him up. After nearly a year of objections – including an incredible attempt by the CHRC to argue that it wouldn't answer various questions for "reasons of national security" – the CHRC agreed to allow its staff to be asked questions about the subject, but for just one day. And even that single day's worth of questioning was to be conducted in secret: the CHRC asked the tribunal to ban reporters from the courtroom, and the tribunal complied.

Secret trials aren't allowed in Canada except in the most extreme situations – for example, when there truly *is* a genuine national security matter being discussed. And on those rare occasions when court publication bans are issued, the ban typically is limited in scope – extending only, say, to the name of minor children. The rest of the trial is still public.

The reason for this is that justice belongs to everyone: The entire country has an interest in seeing Canada's laws being applied fairly. Courts don't deal with cases merely to satisfy the specific interests of the parties involved; they run trials to establish legal precedents for the entire country and to send a moral message concerning what's right and what's wrong. Judges have a self-interested reason for ensuring the transparency of their trials too: open proceedings help build public confidence in the workings of the justice system.

In the past when human rights tribunal hearings were ordered to be held in secret, the CHRC's targets couldn't do anything about it – since most lacked the means to challenge the agency's decisions. That changed in 2008, when mighty *Maclean's* magazine, pricked into action after being hit with a few hate speech complaints itself, decided to take a larger interest in the commission's censorious methods. Lemire's hearing on March 25 was of particular interest to *Maclean's* and its readers: for the first time, CHRC staff themselves would be grilled about their tactics. So the magazine sent in Canada's top media lawyer, Julian Porter, who made a legal application to open the hearing to the public. The CHRC opposed the application, but *Maclean's* prevailed.

For the first time ever, a hate speech trial was packed – and not just with mainstream journalists, but with bloggers who'd been following the issue in the wake of the *Maclean's* controversy. Even then, the CHRC tried to obscure the day's proceedings: the commission hired a stenographer to record testimony, but, in an unprecedented move, it refused to publicly release the transcript. (A copy of that transcript eventually was leaked to a journalist, but with an embarrassing admission made at the trial omitted.)

The March 25 hearing was a disaster for the CHRC. Its staff had to admit, under oath, that they routinely went online under false identities to provoke reactions from neo-Nazis. The CHRC admitted that it had no controls over who had access to these CHRC neo-Nazi website membership accounts. Despite dozens of objections made by CHRC lawyers – apparently to run out the clock on the one-day hearing – the CHRC's dirty laundry was aired in the national media.

The dirtiest fact of all: the CHRC had logged on to a neo-Nazi website by illegally hacking into a private citizen's wireless Internet account at her home. It was a means to cover the CHRC's tracks, so that the identity of the originating, government computers would be hidden. That staggering revelation came from Alain Monfette, a Bell Canada security officer, who had been subpoenaed by Lemire to find out who had gone online as "Jadewarr," one of the CHRC's neo-Nazi codenames. Monfette disclosed to a stunned courtroom that Jadewarr's posts had been made through the Internet account of Nelly Hechme, a young woman whose wi-fi-enabled apartment was around the corner from the CHRC's offices. She was absolutely shocked to learn that her wireless Internet network had been hacked – and that the hacking was associated with neo-Nazi activities.

If the CHRC had gotten its way, the news of the hacking would never have been made public. Hechme was told of her unwitting role as a conduit between government snoops and neo-Nazi websites by a reporter, not the CHRC, which was quite content to let her remain unaware.

Hechme hired a lawyer and promptly brought a complaint to Canada's privacy commissioner, who immediately began an investigation of the CHRC. The Ottawa Police Service investigated the matter too, and referred the file to the RCMP's high-tech crimes division.

This was a welcome departure from prior practice. In the past, not only has the CHRC escaped scrutiny from the RCMP and local constabularies, but the commission has somehow convinced several Canadian police forces to actually participate in its amateur-hour investigations. In some cases, for instance, police have improperly handed over to the CHRC confidential evidence acquired in police raids using criminal search warrants. That's a sign that the sloppy, unethical practices of the CHRC are spreading, infecting real police forces. And it's not just a political embarrassment – it's a real and pressing danger to the rule of law and public safety.

In fact, at Lemire's March 25, 2008, hearing, Dean Steacy, one of the CHRC's hate investigators – who also happened to be a user of the Jadewarr neo-Nazi identity – confessed under oath to simply phoning up police departments and asking for things from their evidence lockers, such as computer hard drives of people the CHRC was targeting.

Steacy was asked: "I take it that your position is that the police department who obtain a search warrant for criminal purposes can simply take that information acquired under a search warrant for that purpose and give it to you on request; correct?"

Steacy's reply: "Yes."

Police search warrants are among the most powerful weapons in the state's arsenal. They legalize what would otherwise be the crimes of breaking and entering and theft. They violate citizens' property rights and even their rights to self-defence. When police come to your house with a warrant to search, they can break down your door if you lock it and can physically restrain you if you try to stop them. Search warrants are easily abused instruments of state power, which is why they're granted by judges only for narrowly defined purposes, and only after government officials have shown some prima facie evidence suggesting that a warrant is needed. But what good are such procedural safeguards if CHRC snoops are effectively allowed to walk into the police evidence locker and take whatever they like?

London, Ontario, police officer Terry Wilson had given Steacy confidential evidence that had been seized from a police raid – a raid that had to be approved in advance by a judge, who authorized the search warrant. Wilson then handed over that seized police evidence to Steacy – who is not a police officer.

In cross-examination Steacy was asked whether he checked whether Wilson had "informed the Justice of the Peace when he got the warrant that he was going to distribute copies of the hard drive to people who asked for it."

"No, I didn't," came the expected reply. Steacy simply asked for it, and Wilson just handed it over. No fuss, no nosy judges to convince.

One can only imagine the red faces among the local men in uniform. Of course no prosecutor would dare to apply for a search warrant if it were known that he or she would share the fruits of the ensuing police raid with anyone who asked for it; no judge would grant it.

The CHRC's shenanigans weren't just bringing disgrace to the agency itself and the police who casually acquiesced to its invasive methods, they were poisoning the well for police who would be seeking legitimate search warrants to go after drug dealers, violent crooks, and other real criminals in the future.

But that didn't trouble Steacy or Wilson. Nor did it trouble the CHRC itself: Steacy remains happily employed at the commission, even after admitting his activities in open court.

It isn't just Wilson who's known to have given confidential police information to the CHRC. Stephen Camp of the Edmonton Police Service – neo-Nazi codename Estate – has done the same thing. He would access the police department's classified criminal information database, called CPIC, and search it at the CHRC's behest. Camp testified that he used "everything from surveillance, computerized checks on motor vehicles [and] directory checks utilizing CPIC" to help the CHRC find its targets. In these cases, there wasn't even a search warrant or an appearance before a judge to act as a fig leaf. Officer Camp simply put the full information-retrieval services of the police at the disposal of civil servants who were spying on the web-surfing habits of private citizens.

There is an old legal maxim that says justice must not only be done, it must be *seen* to be done. Canada's HRCs have set Canada back in regard to both objectives. Their lawless practices have not only undermined centuries-old principles of due process and natural justice, they have eroded public confidence in the rule of law. They have brought the administration of justice into disrepute, and have turned legitimate police forces into political tools. And amazingly, they've done so without most Canadians noticing.

Thankfully, that is changing. Canadians are beginning to wake up.

Chapter 3
HOW COULD WE LET THIS HAPPEN?

So far, I have focused on how human rights commissions lost their way. They are no longer shields that protect people, but swords that take their civil rights away. The question I'm hoping many readers now are asking themselves is, how could we let this happen? In a society that is otherwise committed to protecting due process for every aspect of the government's relationship with its citizens, how could Canadians have permitted these taxpayer-funded star chambers to trample our basic civil liberties?

A large part of the answer, I believe, lies in the emotional power of those two words *human rights*. Anything done in the name of human rights, from the United Nations to our own human rights commissions, seems to automatically get a free pass from Canadian journalists and politicians alike.

How did you feel on the morning of September 11, 2001, when you first heard of the terrorist attacks on New York and

Washington? Shocked? Angry? Perhaps more than anything, scared? Was the hijacking of four airliners and the murder of thousand of innocents just the beginning? Would they attack Canada too?

That's how lots of people felt – including the workforce at Kinexus Bioinformatics Corporation. Kinexus is a high-tech company based in Vancouver. In the fall of 2000, they hired an employee named Ghassan Asad, a single man in his thirties who had just immigrated from Saudi Arabia. He regularly talked about his dislike for the United States and was constantly getting calls from the Middle East on his cellphone.

In September 2001, when Asad became a citizen and finally got a Canadian passport, he announced that he was going on a trip to the United States, by himself – including to New York City and Washington, D.C. He returned with photos of the White House, the U.S. Capitol, and the Twin Towers, taken with the new camera he'd bought just for the trip. He showed off those pictures around the office – and even published them in the company newsletter on September 7. He called his World Trade Center photos "special."

On the morning of September 11, 2001, Kinexus's staff were in shock about the news coming from the United States. Except Asad. According to co-workers, he seemed light-hearted, happy, even jovial. His closest friend at the office – a young receptionist called Patricia Stoute, with whom he would often go out to dinner and clubs – testified that Asad defended Palestinians who were shown on TV dancing jubilantly at the news of the terrorist attacks.

Another co-worker, Asad's friend Catherine Sutter, testified that on 9/11, Asad had remarked on the "strength and resolve" of the terrorists who flew the jets, and that he had brought out his World Trade Center photos to show everyone again. Still another co-worker, Mira Karia, testified that Asad joked about the "coincidence" of him being in New York and Washington just days earlier, and that some people might think he was a "terrorist." Stoute said he also joked about being "a spy."

Within hours, it was reported that the attacks were perpetrated by radical Muslim terrorists. Later, news reports said fifteen of the nineteen hijackers were young, single men from Saudi Arabia, some of whom had visited America extensively in the months before the attacks and even trained there as pilots.

Imagine you had been working at Kinexus in that raw first week after the attacks, with a young Saudi male who hated America and who had just come back from a trip to New York and Washington. What would you think? And what would you do?

His friend Patricia Stoute started remembering a lot of troubling details: a comment from Asad that he wanted to learn how to fly a plane; Asad's reclusive roommate, who moved out shortly before 9/11; the confrontation that Asad had with a Canadian border guard when he was returning to Canada from his trip. Stoute talked with her sister, Heather, about her suspicions. Heather knew someone at the RCMP, and passed his phone number on to her sister. Stoute made a confidential phone call and related what she knew. The RCMP told her that she'd done the right thing.

On September 17, plainclothes RCMP visited Kinexus and discreetly asked to meet with Asad in the boardroom. The next morning, they called him down to the police station and interviewed him again. Then they interviewed him a third time, this time on videotape, and asked for copies of his U.S. vacation pictures. They asked him about his political and religious beliefs, and if he had ever met Osama bin Laden. Asad answered the questions and lent them his camera. In the end, Asad was never linked to any wrongdoing: All of the accumulated details amounted to nothing more than coincidence.

But the fact that Asad didn't return to work for a week and a half added to the climate of suspicion at the office. When he finally returned to work, he spoke to his friend Catherine Sutter and told her that he wanted to know the name of the Kinexus employee who had called the police. She told him to move on – that everyone had calmed down and that he should "forgive" the person who called in the tip. He said he wouldn't until he'd received an apology. For the rest of his time at the company, he kept demanding that name.

Sutter suggested Asad clear the air by writing another story in the company newsletter, and Asad agreed that this would be a good idea. He wrote that he had been interviewed by the RCMP and said they were done with him. "Now I have put it behind me and am going forward. If anyone has any questions, please feel free to talk to me about it (absolutely!). Also I would like to thank everyone who called me at home to offer their support during this difficult time."

At the office, things started to normalize. If his co-workers still harboured suspicions, these didn't affect his place at the company. He continued to receive pay raises and was promoted to manager.

But Asad just wouldn't let go of the fact that one of his co-workers had been so nervous about him in the immediate aftermath of 9/11 that this colleague had called the police. He stopped attending company social events, saying he refused to break bread with someone who had it in for him. He was stressed but refused to take his doctor's prescriptions for medication to help him cope. He spent more and more time with Sutter, who tried to be his personal life coach. He started bickering with management. He demanded a one-month vacation – to go back to the Middle East.

Asad became more and more focused on rooting out his perceived enemy. He began a sort of work-to-rule campaign, refusing to fill out key forms that the company needed to report to its investors. In March 2003 – fully eighteen months after 9/11 – the company ran out of patience. Asad, then a manager, was fired by Kinexus, for cause.

Readers can guess what came next: Asad went to the B.C. Human Rights Tribunal, demanding $90,000 from Kinexus. Asad called his co-workers – including a black woman and a Hindu woman – racist. He called the boss of Kinexus, the one who promoted him after 9/11, racist. He even called Kinexus *itself* racist, though most of its staff and management were minorities. Other Muslims worked there, including one who used the boardroom every day for prayers.

At his human rights trial, which lasted twenty-six days, Asad admitted that he had never experienced any racism at the company before. He described his relationship with his co-workers and managers before 9/11 as "the best. Couldn't be better." He even admitted that he "could understand" why the RCMP interviewed him about his trip. But he just wouldn't accept the fact that a co-worker had been scared of him. Enraged by this fact, he kept returning again and again to the blanket charge that he was surrounded by racists.

In the end, Asad won – sort of. The B.C. Human Rights Tribunal didn't convict Kinexus of firing Asad for racist reasons. "The evidence has led me to conclude," said tribunal chair Abraham Okazaki, "albeit with difficulty, that Mr. Asad's termination was not because of his race, religion, place of origin, or political belief." Kinexus was convicted of "discriminat[ing] against a person regarding employment."

Huh? How could the tribunal find that Kinexus discriminated against Asad "regarding employment" when it also acknowledged, however grudgingly, that he'd been promoted and paid well (Okazaki found that Asad had received the largest pay raise in the whole company) and that his eventual termination was the result of his own misbehaviour?

According to the BCHRT, the villain was Patricia Stoute. By making that call to the RCMP, Okazaki reasoned, she had turned Kinexus into a "racist" workplace. The tribunal chair mentioned – with obvious regret – that Stoute had not been personally named in the complaint, so the only entity that could be fined was Kinexus, which had to fork over a five-figure payout. Okazaki actually stated that he wished Asad had sued for *more*.

Seven years after 9/11, with the benefit of seven years of hindsight, Okazaki – a man with no expertise in security or risk analysis or any other relevant field – decided that Stoute's suspicions were unfounded. This made Stoute, in his mind, a racist.

It might well be that Stoute was wrong about Asad. The RCMP seems to think so – but only after interviewing Asad no fewer than three times. And Okazaki doesn't know what they asked, and what they heard, and what else they know. If Stoute's complaint was so absurd, why did the RCMP feel it necessary to be so thorough?

But even if Stoute *was* completely off base in her complaint to the RCMP, what business is that of the BCHRT? Since when do good-faith calls to the police have to meet some test for political correctness? So the BCHRT thought terrified citizens should be punished for reporting suspicious activities days after the biggest terrorist attack on North American soil – despite the police invitation to do so?

"Individuals do have a societal duty to report to the police what they reasonably believe to be the commission of a crime," Okazaki conceded. But "they are under no such duty," he added, "if their suspicions are based on prejudice rooted in racial profiling, and inflated by unfounded speculation, assumptions and exaggerations." Racial profiling? The man was a Saudi immigrant who talked about his hatred for America and flew down to the World Trade Center and White House just before 9/11. Even without any consideration of the man's race or religion, these details properly raised red flags.

To the extent that Stoute made "assumptions," they resulted from the same sort of mental process that most people undertake when they look out for criminal activity: matching a person's behaviour and other characteristics to that of known criminals. If such basic mental tools of deduction are now illegal, we'd better shut down Crime Stoppers, hadn't we? Or better yet, keep the service running, and use it to entrap citizens into human rights violations.

What's particularly ridiculous about the story is this: even if Stoute were a raging bigot, the case still wouldn't amount to employment discrimination. Stoute wasn't Asad's boss. She had no power over his pay or his career trajectory. She apparently was his closest friend – other than the roommate who moved out right before 9/11. The two of them went out for dinner dates and to clubs – although that stopped after 9/11. She didn't discriminate against Asad in any way, and had no power to do so in the work context even if she had wanted to.

This is a case about a woman who became scared in the shadow of a major terrorist attack, and performed her civic duty by reporting to the police the risk, however remote, that someone in her midst might be plotting more of the same. By punishing the employer of the person who performed this civic duty, the BCHRT did more than monetarily victimize an innocent employer; it also sent a chill through every private citizen with information to report to the authorities.

Somewhere in Canada, there really may be people plotting horrible things. Are their friends, neighbours, and co-workers going to report them if they know that the government's primary interest is shooting the "racist" messenger?

It may seem shocking to you that human rights commissions would put the hurt feelings of a disgruntled worker above the rights of Canada's citizens to national security. But after my years of research in this field, I can't say that it surprises me one bit. One of the themes that consistently jumps out at me is the obsessive manner in which human rights mandarins pursue their dogmas. In their minds, the fight against discrimination (as they define the term) seems to be so important that it overrides every other problem and challenge facing our society – including, shockingly, the mental health needs of rape victims.

In 1995, a male-to-female transsexual called Kimberly Nixon applied to volunteer as a rape crisis counsellor at the Vancouver Rape Relief (VRR) centre. VRR turned Nixon down. For entirely understandable reasons, only women are allowed to counsel rape victims at VRR (and many similar facilities). Although Kimberly Nixon had undergone sex change surgery, and Nixon's birth certificate had been changed by the B.C. government to say "F" instead of "M," VRR felt that the six-foot-tall athlete, even with plenty of makeup, still looked like he had been born a man. It is an undisputed medical fact that many women suffer post-traumatic stress disorder after a rape. In many cases, merely *seeing* a man at close quarters can trigger a flashback and other forms of psychological trauma. The crisis centre felt that rape victims would not want to be confronted with someone who looks like (and genetically still is) a man in a rape crisis safe house – let alone confide their problems to that person.

VRR did the best it could to accommodate Nixon's desire to help the cause. They invited him to join their fundraising committee. That way, he'd be able to help rape victims without violating the spirit of VRR's women-only counselling policy. But Nixon refused. His goal, he said, was "to give something back" to women now that he considered himself one of them. But what Nixon really wanted was to satisfy his own psychological needs, not theirs; being permitted to move freely among women in their most vulnerable state would provide the ultimate validation that he'd officially entered the sisterhood.

The day after Nixon was rejected as a volunteer counsellor by VRR, he filed a human rights complaint, claiming that they'd discriminated against him based on his sex. VRR immediately apologized to Nixon; they even offered him money for his "hurt feelings." But they would not bend on their women-only policy.

It took more than five years for the matter to get to trial – a twenty-one-day hearing that cost VRR more than $150,000, money that otherwise would have gone to helping rape victims. Nixon didn't talk a lot about the women the VRR served. Instead, he talked about himself, and his own feelings, and his human right to be a rape crisis counsellor at VRR, whether they wanted him or not.

And he won.

Heather MacNaughton, the same tribunal member who later would preside over the trial of Mark Steyn and *Maclean's* magazine, dismissed VRR's arguments as selfish. MacNaughton had listened to the testimony of Edith Swain, a rape victim who said that, had she been forced to deal with Nixon, she would not have gone to VRR. Swain said she would have "felt uncomfortable," and "would not have confided" in him. Yet MacNaughton ruled that "Ms. Swain's evidence was not particularly persuasive."

"The actions of Rape Relief impacted the dignity of Ms. Nixon," MacNaughton declared, "and denied her the opportunity to participate fully and freely in the economic, social, political and cultural life of British Columbia." This is complete nonsense, of course. Does this mean that those of us who go through life without counselling raped women lead empty lives bereft of "economic, social, political and cultural" engagement with the society around us?

And then the victim card: "[VRR] failed to take into account Ms. Nixon's already disadvantaged position within Canadian society as a member of a group that has been marginalized," MacNaughton wrote in her seventy-page judgment.

Ending Nixon's "marginalization" trumped VRR's pledge to help raped women. VRR, MacNaughton ruled, "did not meet its obligation to accommodate Ms. Nixon to the point of undue hardship." You'd think the women who fled to VRR had already put up with enough "hardship" themselves without having to act as gender-affirming therapists for a troubled man. But MacNaughton thought differently. She ordered VRR to immediately start allowing men-turned-women such as Nixon to work at VRR. And she ordered VRR to pay Nixon the largest cash award for "pain and suffering" that had ever been awarded by the B.C. Human Rights Tribunal up until that time.

MacNaughton's order caused a public uproar because it was seen as re-victimizing rape victims. VRR spent its precious funds to appeal the case to a real court, which overturned MacNaughton's ruling. Nixon appealed that court's decision to the B.C. Court of Appeal. Again, VRR won; again, Nixon appealed, this time to the Supreme Court of Canada, which refused to hear the case. After ten years of expensive litigation, VRR had finally won.

There are real human rights, such as the right to be free from violence. And then there are fake human rights, such the right of a transsexual to work in a rape crisis shelter as a form of homemade therapy. But Canada's human rights industry doesn't seem to know the difference.

If British Columbia sounds to you like the land that common sense forgot when it comes to human rights, you're right. Many of the most ridiculous case studies discussed in this book originate in that province.

Take, for instance, the time the B.C. Human Rights Tribunal declared that a McDonald's restaurant employee had the human right not to wash her hands, even when she worked in the kitchen, and instead should be accommodated by finding her another job in the organization where hand-washing was not essential. In theory this makes sense; but in practice, McDonald's, who ought to know, say that there aren't any positions that don't require handwashing.

Beena Datt was a McDonald's employee who claimed she'd developed a skin condition that prevented her from washing her hands in compliance with McDonald's hygiene policy. That's the same hygiene policy that has helped turn McDonald's into a fast-food market leader here in the West and an embassy for Westerners travelling overseas. When you're in a Third World country and tired of eating in hygiene-challenged local restaurants, you can count on a Western standard of cleanliness at McDonald's.

Which is to say that McDonald's handwashing policy isn't just a matter of corporate pride, it's a key to its business model.

In British Columbia, it's also a legal matter: Both the Health Act and its Food Premises Regulation mandate rigorous hygiene policies. And then there's the food protection guidelines issued by the B.C. Centre for Disease Control. McDonald's follows all of them.

No matter what you think of Big Macs and Quarter Pounders, you've got to concede that the folks at McDonald's are clean freaks. Their rules not only require employees to wash their hands after using the bathroom, but also after shaking someone's hand, after taking food out of the freezer, or after touching a door handle. They even have a little bell that goes off every hour to remind employees to all go wash their hands.

But Datt said she wouldn't wash her hands – at least not more than once in a while. She said it hurt too much. McDonald's tried to help. They gave her two months of disability leave, while Datt tried out different creams and lotions to alleviate her skin condition. She came back to work, but her hands started hurting again when she washed them.

Again, McDonald's gave her disability pay, as different doctors tried to solve Datt's condition, even checking her for exotic allergies. After two and a half years of disability leave punctuated by two more failed attempts to start working again, it became clear that Datt simply couldn't do any of the jobs at McDonald's that required food handling. Finally, McDonald's let her go.

Other people might have moved on, looking for work where handwashing wasn't required. But not Datt. She sued McDonald's. Not for wrongful dismissal – handwashing was clearly a legitimate requirement of the job. Nor for reneging on the payment of disability insurance – McDonald's certainly had been generous with that. In fact, Datt didn't really sue the restaurant chain at all in the normal sense of the word, for they clearly had lived up to their employment obligations, and then some. Rather, Datt went to the people she knew would give her the kind of complaint-friendly "justice" she wanted: the B.C. Human Rights Tribunal. And there she met a former divorce lawyer and left-wing lobbyist named Judy Parrack.

Parrack ruled that there was no evidence about whether Datt could function at McDonald's if she washed her hands less often.

Parrack was up and away, socking it to the big, evil corporation on behalf of a poor working woman. She ordered McDonald's to pay Datt $23,000 for "lost income" and an additional $25,000 for her "dignity and self-respect." The tribunal found no evidence that McDonald's treated Datt disrespectfully other than the alleged violation of her right not to wash her hands as often as McDonald's required. But that, apparently, was beside the point. According to the B.C. Human Rights Tribunal, a kitchen worker's self-respect trumps a company's commitment to cleanliness. They violated her human rights. So McDonald's was ordered to pay $50,000 plus interest.

Parrack ruled that McDonald's just didn't do enough to accommodate their long-time employee. McDonald's answer was simple: there was no job in the restaurant, including the manager, who wasn't expected to handle food from time to time. There just wasn't any reasonable way to keep on an employee who couldn't or wouldn't wash her hands as often as required. That wasn't good enough for Parrack. So fifty grand it was.

But from the company's perspective, even that outrageous penalty – plus two years of disability payments, plus three years of legal fees – wasn't the worst of it. Nor was the tribunal's invention of a standard for McDonald's that was less stringent than McDonald's required. No, it was the BCHRT's order that McDonald's "cease the discriminatory conduct or any similar conduct and refrain from committing the same or similar contravention." Beena Datt and her unwashed hands no longer toil under the Golden Arches. But since the order applies to any future case similar to Datt's, dozens of other fry jockeys could be emboldened to pass up soap and water under cover of human rights.

What would happen if, heaven forbid, someone contracted a disease from McDonald's food because of this insane order? Could the victim sue the restaurant for failing to live up to its legal public health requirements, even though McDonald's *wanted* to do so? Could the BCHRT itself be sued? What if it wasn't just one customer who got an upset stomach, but a dozen people dying from *E. coli?* And why do we have to play such a risky game in any case, when the science behind food hygiene is settled?

The McDonald's decision, as appalling as it is, is not unique. In a 2004 ruling by Alberta's human rights commission, Ruby Repas won an equally outrageous – albeit substantially less generous – cash payment from Albert's Family Restaurant. She had been working as the kitchen manager there when she was fired after contracting incurable hepatitis. She won $5,000 in vindication of her human right to not be required to wash her hands.

How will these cases affect the decision making of restaurant managers faced with stubbornly germ-ridden employees? Do they risk their customers' health by keeping such workers on the job or do they risk a fine of $50,000 or $100,000 at the hands of an HRC?

It's something to think about during your next trip to the drive-thru.

For a $9.75/hour burger-flipper such as Beena Datt, $50,000 was a lot of money. The large payouts awarded by HRCs appear to have given rise to a new job category: the professional human rights complainant.

Take the case of a frequently complaining police cadet who was recently awarded $500,000 because he got yelled at by his drill sergeant at the academy. Ali Tahmourpour is a Muslim man born in Iran. In a tolerant country such as Canada, thankfully, most people don't care where you were born or about the nature of your religious beliefs. But a settlement such as the one mentioned above would open the door to people who might be professional human rights complainants.

When he was in his early twenties, Tahmourpour went to work for Revenue Canada as a student customs inspector. The agency offered to keep him on, but Tahmourpour filed a human rights complaint, saying he was harassed and given unfair performance appraisals. He spent three years fighting that complaint until it was finally thrown out by the Federal Court of Appeal. That was his test run.

The following year, he signed up for the RCMP's police academy in Regina, claiming it was his lifelong dream to become an RCMP officer. I wonder if the Mounties had phoned Revenue Canada for references.

After just twelve weeks at the police academy, Tahmourpour washed out. When Tahmourpour received word that he had failed boot camp, he "began behaving very strangely" according to his classmates, who had to escort him to the academy's infirmary twice when he was "vomiting, shaking, hyperventilating and was incoherent." An RCMP psychologist diagnosed him as passively suicidal. Three of his fellow cadets later testified that "they would be afraid to work with him in the field." In fact, his conduct was so erratic that the RCMP put a note on his file barring him from reapplying.

Tahmourpour complained to the Canadian Human Rights Commission, which rejected his case. He appealed that ruling to the Federal Court; they also rejected his case. Again he appealed, and he was granted a second human rights hearing. After eight years of quarrelling, Tahmourpour finally got his payday: $500,000 in back pay and pain and suffering, plus reinstatement in the RCMP's training academy.

The RCMP have announced they're appealing the decision, again.

The Canadian Human Rights Tribunal acknowledges that "there was credible evidence that Mr. Tahmourpour had difficulty performing competently in scenarios, and that this was largely a function of his inability to listen to people, to integrate the information he received and to formulate an appropriate course of action based on that information." The phrase *his inability to integrate information* is a very gentle way of saying Tahmourpour wasn't too bright.

The Mounties surely have spent far more than $500,000 on lawyers already, so their concern clearly isn't just about the money. The RCMP is fighting this case on principle. Simply put, the RCMP doesn't want to risk the integrity of its police force by training an unfit candidate who, carrying a badge and gun, might pose a danger to the Canadian public.

As he had done at his previous job, Tahmourpour accused the RCMP of racism. But in none of the 267 paragraphs of the tribunal's decision is there any clear evidence of racism. There are, however, plenty of descriptions of instances in which Tahmourpour seemed to be baiting his instructors – and his fellow classmates – with his minority status.

On one occasion, Tahmourpour requested permission from his drill instructor to wear an amulet, in violation of the police academy's rule against all jewellery (even watches were forbidden). Tahmourpour claimed the amulet had religious significance (which would come as news to the rest of the world's Muslims), and he insisted that an exception be made for him. And he got it: no crosses, stars of David, or kirpans were allowed during the cadets' training, but Tamourpour was given permission to wear his amulet.

Yet when his drill sergeant publicly mentioned his request for an exception, Tahmourpour claimed racism. The tribunal agreed, ruling that "the RCMP Dress and Hygiene Instructions, and the announcement made by Sergeant Hébert in front of Troop 4, adversely differentiated against him on the basis of his religion."

That's a pretty impressive sentence, when you read it slowly. If the RCMP didn't allow Tahmourpour to wear his "religious" pendant, it would be discrimination. But if they *did* allow him to wear it – an exception that would surely draw attention and criticism from fellow cadets – the sergeant couldn't mention it, or that would be discrimination too.

Tahmourpour seemed to go out of his way to entrap his trainers in weird discussions about his ethnicity. When signing a document in front of an instructor, Tahmourpour chose to write his signature in Persian, from right to left, and ended it with an artistic embellishment. The startled instructor asked Tahmourpour what language he was signing, and if it was indeed his real signature. The tribunal spent an enormous amount of time on this piece of trivia, and concluded that the instructor's question about the signature was "a derogatory comment" that was "based on a prohibited ground of discrimination."

And on and on it went. Tahmourpour claimed that the firearms instructor shouted at him. This was freely confessed to by the firearms instructor, who said he shouted all the time. It was a firing range, after all – a noisy and dangerous place.

Constable Brendon McCarney, another visible minority at the academy with Tahmourpour, didn't much like the firearms instructor either, telling the tribunal "he was confrontational; he would yell at the cadets right in their faces, very close to them." The first time it happened to him, McCarney "was stunned," but he "did not repeat the mistake that prompted the reaction." That's pretty much the result an instructor would want when the lesson being taught involves guns. And it was by no means reserved for Tahmourpour. According to McCarney, "anyone who made a mistake was yelled at by [the instructor,] Corporal [Dan] Boyer, including Caucasian cadets."

No instructor had ever uttered a racist word toward Tahmourpour. True, one called him a "loser," a "coward," and "incompetent." Those words may or may not have been fair – the testimony of his fellow cadets suggests they were – but there's nothing about Islam, Iran, or skin colour in those generic insults. They're pretty much what you'd get if you called down to central casting and ordered up any kind of police or military drill sergeant: a hard-edged perfectionist whose tough love would one day save the lives of his cadets.

But that's not what the Tribunal saw. Karen Jensen, the tribunal chair, wrote that "Corporal Boyer denied that he was racist; he has many friends and family members who are from visible minority groups. However . . . it is quite possible that

Corporal Boyer's attitudes with respect to visible minority cadets and RCMP officers are markedly different from his attitudes towards his friends and family."

There was no proof of racial discrimination at all – in fact, there was plenty of proof to the contrary. But when you're a lifelong anti-racism activist given the power of a court order, you find ways to see racism in even the purest of hearts.

Jensen pointed to a survey that showed 51 per cent of white males in the RCMP thought that hiring quotas for women and minorities gave those groups an unfair advantage. Since giving these groups an arbitrary leg up is, in fact, the explicit purpose of affirmative action, that statistic is hardly scandalous. (In fact, it's hard to understand why the percentage is so low.) But Jensen seized on it anyway to do a little racial stereotyping herself. Corporal Boyer's "behaviour toward Mr. Tahmourpour," she concluded, "may have been based, at least in part, on resentment that he, like many regular Caucasian Males, felt towards members of visible minority groups and women in the RCMP."

Note the word *may* in this last sentence. There was no evidence that Corporal Boyer felt "resentment" toward minorities in general, or Tahmourpour in particular. But because some other white men told a survey they felt reverse discrimination was unfair, that was enough to infer that Boyer, as a white man, had racism in his heart when he shouted at Tahmourpour or asked him about his Persian signature. This was part of a pattern in Jensen's decision: every criticism of Tahmourpour was spun as a racist act; while every failure on the complainant's part was ascribed to the stress of working amid such racism.

All of which made Tahmourpour's demands seem odd: He asked for a big cash payment – but also had the gall to ask to be "immediately instated as a regular RCMP officer," at the same level of seniority and pay as the other cadets who were in the training academy with him. If the RCMP academy really was such a den of racism, why would he want to get back there so quickly?

The tribunal's assessment of the RCMP was based on circumstantial evidence, wild extrapolations, and plain old prejudice. But even as biased as it was, the tribunal couldn't help but note Tahmourpour's flaws. Jensen called Tahmourpour "evasive," and described his answers as "unclear, contradictory and hard to follow." She also described some of his comments as "implausible" – such as his claim that instructors demanded meetings with him every day at lunch, so that he would grow weak from hunger. (When asked how this squared with his weight gain, Tahmourpour said he bought a lot of snacks from Wal-Mart.)

One of the creepiest insights into Tahmourpour was when he gave the tribunal a transcript of a phone conversation with one of his fellow cadets that he had taped, in which Tahmourpour tried to get his colleague to dish up dirt on the academy. It didn't work – other than to give insight into how Tahmourpour treated his friends.

Would Tahmourpour really have been a crack RCMP officer? His fellow cadets didn't think so. His instructors didn't think so. The RCMP's psychologist didn't think so. When he was kicked out, he went on welfare. He enrolled in a real estate course but quit after selling just one property. He became accredited to be an English/Persian translator but quit after earning just $100. For eight years, Tahmourpour fulfilled the low expectations of everyone who had come into contact with him during those short weeks at the RCMP's academy. The firearms instructor was right: Tahmourpour was a loser.

But Karen Jensen of the Canadian Human Rights Tribunal made him a winner – she ordered the RCMP to pay Tahmourpour $500,000 for his lost career; $9,000 for "pain and suffering"; $12,000 because the racism he faced was "reckless"; and, just to rub it in, $9,500 for Tahmourpour's wasted real estate course.

Then Jensen went further: she ordered Tahmourpour, now thirty-five, to be admitted to the next class of cadets. And she ordered the RCMP to "prevent the discrimination . . . from occurring again." She didn't outline the details of how that ought to be effected. Rather, she ordered the RCMP and Tahmourpour to "reach an agreement" on implementing her vague order, with a warning that if the RCMP didn't come to terms with Tahmourpour on "systemic" changes, she'd come back and force a solution upon them.

It's hard to know what words to use to describe what happened to the RCMP. Perhaps a criminal metaphor is most apt: they were mugged.

What do you call a system that weighs to a nicety the degree of swearing and shouting that is legally permissible during the training of police at a firing range? What message have we sent to the other cadets who failed – and to those who worked hard and had the character and ability to succeed – when someone so obviously ill-equipped for life as a Mountie is foisted upon that weary organization by fiat?

Human rights commissions don't just go after the big fish – multinationals such as McDonald's or government agencies such as the RCMP, which can afford lengthy legal fights and six-figure fines. Those are the cases we hear about, because respondents with deep pockets have the ability to fight back. But most human rights complaints – more than 90 per cent – never make it to a hearing, because the targets collapse under the cost of defending themselves, not to mention the stress.

That's exactly what happened to Ted Kindos, the proprietor of Gator Ted's, a pub in Burlington, Ontario. Kindos is a typical small entrepreneur: He knows a lot about running his business, but he doesn't have a lot of extra time or money to fight busybody government agencies. That makes him a sitting duck for a human rights complaint.

Twenty years ago, a man named Steve Gibson suffered a neck injury that, he claims, left him with a long-term disability – a condition he medicates with marijuana. Gibson likes spending his plentiful free time at Gator Ted's, and he likes to smoke his marijuana there, right in the doorway, for the other customers to enjoy on a second-hand basis – or not. Mainly not.

Gator Ted's other customers say that Gibson doesn't just smoke his marijuana – he flaunts it. He also shows off his government-issued "licence to smoke" for all to see. The way they tell it, Gibson isn't just quietly engaging in self-medication. He's putting on a show, forcing everyone to watch him and smell his smoke.

Even marijuana activists such as Marc Emery, Canada's self-described "prince of pot," think Gibson is simply showing bad manners. "I don't see people with insulin bringing their syringes out in the middle of restaurants and giving themselves injections," said Emery. If pain relief were Gibson's only goal, Emery says, he could simply ingest marijuana in an alcoholic tincture. But then nobody would be watching the Steve Gibson Show.

Parents have complained to Kindos about having to walk by

Gibson's antics with their kids. Truck drivers have complained too, saying that Gibson's smoke might affect their random drug testing at work.

So Kindos asked Gibson to move away from the door. And Gibson launched a complaint with the Ontario Human Rights Commission. Now Kindos had a difficult decision to make: fight or settle. "If this thing goes to the [human rights] tribunal, that's it, we're done. Our restaurant is done," he said. He already had a heart attack at age thirty-eight, and while Gibson is permanently stress-free because of his marijuana medication, Kindos's blood pressure is way up. "We've already been told we can't win," he says.

That's true: in a bizarre move, Afroze Edwards, a spokesperson for the Ontario Human Rights Commission, as much as announced that Kindos was going to lose, telling a Toronto newspaper that Gibson had a disability and thus had a right to "reasonable accommodation" by Gator Ted's. Real courts, of course, don't announce the verdict before the trial has begun.

Losing at the tribunal wouldn't just mean that Gibson gets to continue smoking his pot at Kindos's door. It would mean that Kindos would have to pay Gibson a fine of $20,000 for having violated his human right to smoke pot. (Gibson says it's not about the money. But he's the one who chose that dollar figure in his complaint, and he's the one who could drop that demand at any time.)

Kindos spent $20,000 on legal fees before his hearing even began, and his lawyers told him it would cost another $60,000 to fight it all the way. Gibson, on the other hand, like all human rights complainants, doesn't have to pay a dime. His bill is paid for by Ontario taxpayers, whether he wins or loses.

So, on the eve of his human rights trial, Kindos surrendered. Rather than face a surefire defeat at the human rights commission, he copped a plea and cut a deal with Gibson.

Neither Kindos nor Gibson revealed the exact nature of the deal – as is typical of out-of-court settlements. (According to Gibson, he got what he originally asked for – presumably the $20,000.) But as it turns out, the details are moot: the provincial liquor control board has deemed the arrangement illegal, thereby sending everybody back to the drawing board. And so, Kindos's legal nightmare continues.

Pot activist Emery has it right. This isn't about the pros or cons of medical marijuana. It's about safeguarding important principles that we're supposed to be able to take for granted in this country – such as the right to private property, and the right of a small business owner to serve his community.

There's a thread that runs through many human rights complaints: the complainers are often the kind of people who feel endlessly put upon by the world around them, and they wile away their productive years on their grievances. When Beena Datt's hands hurt from washing them, she didn't find a new job – she spent two and a half years on "disability" leave instead, and another few years suing about it. Ali Tahmourpour has wasted eight of the best years of his life complaining about twelve rough weeks at cadet school back in the 1990s. And Steve Gibson's neck pain wasn't just a reason for him to stop working – it's an excuse to liberate $20,000 from the poor shmoe who runs the pub down the street.

There is no denying that, even in these cases, human rights commissions are trying to resolve some real underlying grievance. Obviously, these complainants had problems with the world. Their feelings were hurt; they were offended. As a result, they concocted elaborate moral narratives that cast themselves as victims. Life isn't always fair or fun. But their problems aren't real human rights complaints, and it wasn't the government's role to get involved.

Human rights commissions are more prone to attract frivolous complaints such as theirs because they lack the procedural barriers that our real courts have developed over the centuries. Thin-skinned people are allowed to file lawsuits in regular courts, of course, but they have to hire their own lawyers first – a potentially expensive proposition. Not so in human rights commissions, where government lawyers prosecute cases using taxpayers' money. In Canada, a lawsuit that goes to two days of trial typically costs the plaintiff about $60,000 in legal fees. It's unlikely that an unemployed, chronic user of marijuana could muster the motivation, let alone the spare cash, to fight for the right to blow pot smoke at fellow bar patrons – he'd probably just take his reefer into the parking lot, as any well-mannered pothead would. But when the government pays for it, why not roll the dice?

Even if they can afford their own lawyers, litigants in real court face risks if they file nuisance suits – if they lose, they're on the hook for the other side's legal fees too. This disincentive is absent at human rights commissions. That's why they've become magnets for the permanently umbraged – misfits who escalate all of life's normal disagreements into bitter legal contests. In a growing number of cases, it is also attracting complainers of fortune, who have cynically turned the human rights legacy of Rosa Parks and the Freedom March into a sort of tax-free slot machine.

It's hard to figure out whether Patricia Sherman is one of the permanently umbraged or a complainer of fortune. She's certainly a bit of a character, even by the colourful standards of Yellowknife, a city full of characters. Sherman is a witch – or, as she prefers to phrase it, "a practising High Priestess." She also has been an animal breeder, a tarot card reader, a school bus driver, a trucker, and a delivery person for the local Boston Pizza. It's that last job that put Sherman in front of a human rights commission – and into this book.

Back in 2004, when the High Priestess was at Boston Pizza waiting for the cooks to give her a set of pies for delivery, she overheard the headbanging rock music the boys were playing in the kitchen. She didn't like it one bit. Sherman is a bit of an old-timer. And the raucous tunes made her lose her Arctic cool. The lyrics were too sexual for her, too bellicose. She argued with the cooks, but they insisted on keeping the music going. The kitchen's hi-fi was their turf. On top of that she said the staff hid the stool she needed to alleviate her back problems.

So Sherman filed a complaint with the Northwest Territories Human Rights Commission, accusing Boston Pizza of among other things sexual harassment. "There was a lot of violent connotations, and it was very pornographic material," Sherman told reporters, referring to the lyrics.

Sherman's description of the music probably was accurate. Rock 'n' roll went sexual when Elvis Presley started wiggling his hips, and it's only got worse since then. It's easy to see how the likes of, say, 2 Live Crew or Rage Against the Machine would be offensive to an older woman, particularly one so passionately attuned to nature's mystical forces.

Brad Baker, the pizza parlour's young night manager, devised a solution worthy of King Solomon himself: the kitchen stereo would be tuned to a radio station – no more CDs.

That solution was implemented in 2005. But Sherman

pressed on with her complaint. The radio row had been settled by a grown-up half Sherman's age. But that wasn't good enough for her: she wanted compensation for sexual harassment and discrimination on the basis of disability. In June 2008, she got $1,000 for her "dignity, feelings and self-respect" and another $2,500 in punitive and exemplary damages. The Northwest Territories Human Rights Commission said that Sherman's testimony was "scattered and unclear," and that the Boston Pizza witnesses were honest and clear.

How did the choice of CDs in a pizza kitchen's stereo rise to the level of human right? If rough language in pop music is now a thought crime, a lot more dominoes are sure to fall.

And that isn't even the craziest part of the story. Thérèse Boullard, the director of the Northwest Territories Human Rights Commission, was asked by reporters about criticisms that Canada's HRCs are indulging wackier and wackier cases. Boullard wouldn't hear of such heresy: "I think quite often what gets reported on are the more extreme cases. What's not reported on are the thousands of more modest cases. The Charter of Rights and Freedoms guarantees equality, and the human rights commissions are one way of realizing that right," she said. Amazingly, the case of Patricia Sherman, was one of those "more modest cases" cited specifically by Boullard. She made a special point of differentiating between her serious work as the Disc Jockey-General for the Arctic and all those other "unreasonable" human rights commission cases in the news these days.

What would lead Boullard – or anyone – to believe that a four-year-old dispute over the music in a kitchen is a legitimate human rights issue? Well, consider that her human rights commission has ten full- and part-time staff on its payroll. To justify the size of her office, she needs enough complaints to keep everyone busy. That's tough in a territory with just forty thousand citizens. Only thirty-six complaints were filed all last year. That's still an enormous number for a territory that, until three years ago, managed to get along just fine without a human rights commission. Of those thirty-six cases, most petered out; only thirteen cases made it to a full hearing last year – that works out to barely one case per staff member per year.

If you're mad about something in your life, no matter how trivial – no matter if it's your own fault – there really is no reason *not* to file a complaint with your unfriendly neighbourhood human rights commission. It doesn't cost you a thing to start a complaint. Not even the price of a postage stamp – you can just fax your complaint in. If you win, you can get tax-free cash, and often some sort of government order that will try to assuage your feelings – like an order to make those darned pizza boys change the CD at work and stop hiding your stool. And even if you lose and the HRC vindicates your opponent, there's the cruel satisfaction of knowing that you've punished your adversaries by putting them through years of legal hassles.

Take the case of Ahmed Assal and his family. In 2000, the Assals moved from Egypt to Halifax. They lived in a couple of different homes before buying a condominium on Willett Street in January 2002. It's a lovely complex of ninety homes, with plenty of green spaces that make it feel like a park. The condo board spends a lot of money on landscaping and other aesthetic touches. The Assals say that's one of the reasons they picked the property. Before they moved in, the Assals reviewed the condominium bylaws carefully. Ahmed even had a lawyer help him. He acknowledges that they saw there was a rule against satellite dishes. But it wasn't a problem: The Assals hadn't had a satellite dish before anyway.

But the next year, the Assals changed their mind. They wanted to set up an ArabSat dish – to get educational programming for the kids, they claimed. It's true that out of the 340 or so channels offered on ArabSat, there are three kids channels – including two described as "Al Jazeera Children's Channels." But the rest of ArabSat's offerings are for grown-ups. There's the Fatwa Channel, for instance – sort of like Court TV, but more exciting. (You never see thieves' hands cut off on Court TV, even during sweeps week.)

And ArabSat carries Al Manar, the official in-house TV channel of the terrorist group Hezbollah. Hassan Fadlallah, Al Manar's news director, once summed up his editorial policy neatly. "We're not looking to interview [former Israeli prime minister Ariel] Sharon. We want to get close to him in order to kill him."

The Assals wrote a letter to the condo board requesting permission to put up a dish. This was a big deal: ArabSat dishes are much larger than the pizza-sized mini-dishes for Canadian satellite TV providers. They're more old-school – big and ugly. And for it to work from the condo complex, an ArabSat dish couldn't simply be bolted to the Assals' own unit – it had to be right out there in the parklike common property, attached to a tree, at just the right angle.

The condo board reviewed the Assals' request and rejected it. No satellite dishes were allowed, period.

But the Assals put the dish up anyway, right in the middle of the common area in the condominium, the very parklike environs that made the condo so attractive to them in the first place. The condo board phoned them to ask them to take it down.

They refused. When other condo owners started complaining, the condo board followed up with a written letter asking the Assals to take the dish down by November 12, 2003.

So the Assals made a pre-emptive strike: on November 5, they sued the condo board. Not in a real court, of course. You don't have to be a lawyer to know that the Assals' claim would have been rejected: they knew about the rule against satellite dishes, they agreed to it, and they violated it. It's called a contract. The condo board would have won, won quickly, and won their costs too. Instead, the Assals took their neighbours to the Nova Scotia Human Rights Commission, alleging that by asking them to take their dish down, their neighbours were engaging in religious discrimination.

Filing the human rights complaint against the condo board wasn't just a trick to put the board on the defensive. It tripped a wire in the Nova Scotia Human Rights Act that served to keep the family from being evicted or sued: Section 11 outlaws what it calls "retaliation" against someone who makes a human rights complaint. By taking their neighbours to a kangaroo court first, the Assals stopped their neighbours from taking them to a real court – or even taking the dish down. Whether the Assals knew in advance that this would be the result of their complaint is unclear. But they found out soon enough – and took advantage of every minute of it.

By the time the Nova Scotia Human Rights Commission finally ruled that the Assals did not, in fact, have a human right to break condo rules so they could watch Al Jazeera, it was April 3, 2007. For three and a half years the case ground its way through the commission, with two commission lawyers working on it at public expense. And for all that time, that hideous mega-dish remained bolted to a tree in the middle of the condominium property.

Human rights commissions say their goal is to increase harmony among Canadians of different backgrounds. Here's a question: Did Nova Scotia's human rights commission, by accepting a complaint that clearly had nothing to do with human rights, *help* race relations? Do you think that hideous ArabSat receiving station, bolted to a tree for three and a half years, made the Assals' eighty-nine neighbours feel better or worse about Canada's multicultural tapestry?

The exact wording of the Nova Scotia HRC's mission statement is "to reduce individual and systemic discrimination in support of a society characterized by equality." But equality means that all the residents at 240 Willett Street are treated the same way – whether they want to put up a dish for ExpressVu, Playboy, or ArabSat. In this case, one family out of ninety got an exception, temporarily – for no other reason than that they played the race card. Because of that provision in Section 11 of their province's Human Rights Act, hundreds of Haligonians now see "human rights" as a cynical codeword for reverse discrimination.

In fact, if someone wanted to deliberately exacerbate racial grievances, it's no exaggeration to say that he or she would be hard-pressed to do a better job than the human rights commissions I've discussed in this chapter. It's like the dinner party line about the Holy Roman Empire being neither holy nor Roman: Human rights commissions have, in effect, become the enemy of human rights – and a variety of other rights besides. As I will explain in the next chapter, this includes the most important right of all: the right to free speech.

Chapter 4

THE TRUE MEANING OF FREE SPEECH

Today's HRCs drum up business by taking on matters that no real court – or tort lawyer, for that matter – would touch. But not just petty matters, such as who gets to decide what music is played in the pizza restaurant kitchen. HRCs tackle matters that are far from petty: complaints that challenge the very foundations of our society, and our nature as free individuals.

One of those foundations is our right to have an opinion or belief that is different from society's orthodoxies, no matter if it's popular, or even correct. That's called freedom of conscience. It's closely related to freedom of speech: having freedom of thought isn't much use if you can't express yourself. These building blocks of Canadian society are so important that we put them right near the beginning of our Charter of Rights and Freedoms, in Section 2, titled "fundamental freedoms":

2. Everyone has the following fundamental freedoms:

a) freedom of conscience and religion;

b) freedom of thought, belief, opinion and expression, including freedom of the press and other media of communication;

c) freedom of peaceful assembly; and

d) freedom of association.

Each one of these fundamental freedoms is under attack by Canada's HRCs, which have started to regulate not just what they call "discriminatory conduct," but also "discriminatory speech."

The biggest HRC in the country is the Canadian Human Rights Commission, headquartered in Ottawa. It has more than two hundred staff and an annual budget in excess of $25 million. It gets its powers from the Canadian Human Rights Act, a law passed by Parliament in 1977.

Section 13 of that law is titled "Hate messages." (In French, it's called "*Propagande haineuse*," which somehow sounds even more Orwellian to my anglo ears.) As many observers predicted when the CHRA became law three decades ago, Section 13 has become an instrument of crude ideological censorship.

The exact wording of Section 13 makes it illegal to say anything over the phone lines or Internet that "is likely to expose a person or persons to hatred or contempt by reason of the fact that that person or those persons are identifiable on the basis of [his group status]."

These words should set off alarm bells in the mind of any civil libertarian. Note, in particular, the fact that one need not actually *incite* hatred to trigger application of the law. One need merely say something that someone feels is "likely" to arouse hatred in the mind of some unidentified third part. It's not a defence if the accused genuinely believes what he or she says, or even if what he or she says is objectively *true*. If, by some chance, HRC bureaucrats believe the words in question might incite hatred, you're guilty.

As Alan Borovoy, general counsel for the Canadian Civil Liberties Association, points out, that's such a vague and subjective test that literally anyone could be caught by it – including documentary filmmakers. By example, Borovoy notes that a movie about the Holocaust could easily be swept up under Section 13, since it could naturally be expected to expose Germans "to hatred or contempt" – just as the story of the Rape of Nanking might elicit a hate reaction toward Japanese people, or a newscast about 9/11 might do the same for people from Saudi Arabia.

The speculative nature of Section 13 reminds me of the blockbuster movie *Minority Report*, in which Tom Cruise's character works as a cop in the department of "pre-crime." He doesn't arrest criminals. He arrests *future* criminals. *Minority Report* is a work of science fiction: the plot revolves around psychics who are able to predict when something bad is going to happen. Section 13 relies instead on human rights tribunals. But in both cases, the concept is the same: It is more or less impossible to plead not guilty if you're charged with a pre-crime. You can't say "I didn't do it." No one said you did *anything*. They said you *might* – in the future. No losses need actually be suffered, so no harm need be proved. This is the main reason why, in the thirty-plus years Section 13 has been on the books, not a single Canadian tried under it has been acquitted.

Section 13 is also creepy in the sense that it seeks to regulate the content of people's minds. Hatred and contempt – the law's targets – are *feelings.* They are negative feelings, to be sure, feelings that we'd probably all like to have less often – and that we'd certainly not want others to have about us. But the fact remains that, in this imperfect world, humans sometimes hold hateful views about some of the people around them. Sometimes, our experiences even cause us to hate whole groups of people – say, lawyers or Scientologists, or telemarketers, or even the Toronto Maple Leafs. A Tutsi tribesman who lost his family to Hutu killers in Rwanda's 1994 genocide may harbour a hatred of all Hutus. Sunni Muslims sometimes hate Shiites – and vice versa.

To criminalize such feelings doesn't just fly in the face of the Canadian Charter of Rights and Freedoms. It's against human nature. You just can't make people turn off their hearts and minds and feel nothing but happiness all the time. In a liberal society, we insist that people desist from acting violently on their negative thoughts, but we don't criminalize the thoughts themselves. We know that hatred is often rooted in feelings of grievance, right or wrong, and that to defuse the hate, you've got to deal with the grievance. You can't just pass a law called the Love Everyone Act.

Real courts govern speech very differently. Our defamation law, for example, is based on a four-hundred-year-old British tradition balancing the right of people to protect their reputations with the right of others to criticize them and the public's right to know. To win a defamation case in Canada, plaintiffs must prove that they were personally identified – not just that they were part of some disparaged "group." And the test is whether their reputation actually suffered damages – not whether it *might,* in the future.

More importantly, truth is an absolute defence in defamation law, no matter how painful the subject matter is. This means, for instance, that libel law could never be used to go after a Christian preacher who declared that the Bible condemns homosexual behaviour as wicked in the eyes of God. (But that preacher could, however, be prosecuted under the Human Rights Act.)

Under the doctrine of "fair comment," libel law also recognizes the right of commentators to express opinions about people – including radical, over-the-top insults. Consider this example: In 1999, Vancouver radio personality Rafe Mair went on air and compared a local Christian activist to Adolf Hitler and the Ku Klux Klan. It's the sort of comment that would make your average human rights commissioner blanch. But in a 9-0 judgment rendered in June 2008, a unanimous Supreme Court of Canada threw out the libel case against Mair, saying that even "outrageous" and "ridiculous" opinions are allowed.

Our highest court understands what common-law nations have recognized for generations: the law allows people to disagree. It doesn't try to sweep their differences and strong emotions under a government-mandated carpet.

But no one is immune from Section 13 – even elected politicians. Jim Pankiw, the former MP for Saskatoon-Humboldt, was hauled before the CHRC to answer for letters he mailed to voters in 2003 expressing his concern about the high prevalence of Aboriginal crime.

There is no disputing that Aboriginal crime rates are high in Saskatchewan and that the law treats Aboriginal criminals differently. Statistics Canada data for 2006 indicate that Aboriginals comprise only about 10 per cent of the population in that province but a whopping 57 per cent of its prison population. There are a dozen possible solutions to the problem, and everyone has a point of view on the subject, from Indian band councils to police chiefs. It's appropriate for a local MP to have an opinion the issue too. And whether it's the right view is for his constituents to decide – not for a bureaucrat in Ottawa.

In 2003, Pankiw mailed tens of thousands of brochures on the subject to his constituents. The mailings had the words *Stop Indian Crime* on the cover and contained statistics demonstrating the elevated incidence of crime in Saskatchewan's Native communities. Nine people complained to the CHRC. Instead of challenging Pankiw in the media or running against him in the next election, they sought to shut him up using Section 13.

Not only did the CHRC take the case, its mandarins fought Pankiw – and Parliament's lawyers – all the way to the Supreme Court, claiming they had the right to investigate what politicians said. (Pankiw lost his appeal, so in late 2008 his case went to a human rights tribunal after all.)

Pankiw was elected by the citizens of Saskatoon; but he didn't win the approval of some unelected bureaucrats in Ottawa. It's quite something when civil servants appointed by elected MPs can then tell those same MPs what they can or can't say. Try that with your boss.

In the end, after two terms in office, Pankiw didn't win re-election in 2004. Whether that was because of his mail-outs or, more likely, because he was no longer affiliated with a political party and ran as an independent, is not known. Either way, it was the voters' decision, and they made it. The fact that a bureaucratic witch hunt against him continues to this day – long after the public has dispatched him – is incredible, and a warning to politicians who would dare to deviate from the CHRC's standards of political correctness.

Pankiw was a public figure commenting on a high-profile issue. But most of the folks who get prosecuted under Section 13 are ordinary Canadians who happen to have controversial opinions. In some especially Orwellian cases, the defendants aren't even people – they're just disembodied electronic identities.

Perhaps the weirdest of these cases was *beachesboy@aol.com v. drumsaremybeat@aol.com*. That's the actual name of the case: in the ultimate postmodern permutation on the concept of human rights, we had two email addresses, not people, duking it out.

If that sounds strange, it is – every other legal action in Canada, from murder trials to traffic tickets, lists the names of the people who are involved. In eight hundred years of our Western legal tradition, stretching back to the Magna Carta, secret accusations were regarded as an affront to justice. Even the Spanish Inquisition was prosecuted by Tomás de Torquemada, in the name of the King and Queen. That's why, in criminal cases, it's always "The Queen" who sues, on behalf of the public interest (in the United States, criminals are charged by "The People"). It's not just common sense, it's a basic principle of natural justice: People who are being sued have the right to face and question their accuser, and know the case against them.

As for beachesboy and drumsaremybeat, they were having an argument about who-knows-what on an AOL chat site; beachesboy got offended, so he complained to the CHRC, which, naturally, got right on the case.

The commission's first order of business was to subpoena AOL's records to find out who drumsaremybeat really was.

CHRC officials spent thousands of dollars in court, and then through private investigators, and narrowed the identity down to the Fleming family of Edmonton – though they weren't quite sure who had gone online using that nickname. So both Mom and Dad Fleming were charged with Section 13 hate speech violations.

The Flemings didn't take the lawsuit too seriously – maybe they thought it was so ridiculous that it had to be a hoax. Or maybe they knew that, no matter how seriously the CHRC took itself, no real court would uphold a judgment against them made by the Tooth Fairy, Santa Claus, or beachesboy.

March 3, 2008, was the big day: the prosecutors and investigators at the CHRC took their case against drumsaremybeat to the Canadian Human Rights Tribunal. It was going to be a high-tech trial for a high-tech crime: the judge of this farce would be in Ottawa, and drumsaremybeat was summoned to a videoconferencing room in Edmonton. The CHRC prosecutors showed up. The CHRT judge showed up. The clerks showed up.

Everybody showed up – except the two nicknamed parties. The whole Canadian human rights war machine was ready for battle, but it was not to be. Karen Jensen, the CHRT chair sitting in Ottawa, phoned the videoconferencing room in Edmonton and asked local personnel to check the lobby to see whether anyone who looked like they might be called drumsaremybeat was hanging around. Beachesboy didn't bother to show up either – even though he filed the complaint in the first place, causing the CHRC to engage in tens of thousands of dollars' worth of investigations and convene a cross-country video hearing. Maybe he slept in. Maybe he was surfing on Lavalife and got so engrossed in a romantic chat that he forgot what time it was. Or maybe beachesboy never existed in the first place.

Whatever the explanation, a lot of high-priced people sat around on the high-priced videoconference call that day, waiting in vain to re-enact some completely meaningless Internet chat forum argument from months past.

It was the only Section 13 case ever brought before the CHRT that didn't result in a conviction – but only because the trial couldn't proceed. To this day, the CHRC refuses to disclose the identity of beachesboy – even though it did all it could to "out" drumsaremybeat as the Flemings.

Virtually identical provisions to Section 13 are found in many provincial human rights laws too, such as Section 3(1) of Alberta's Human Rights, Citizenship and Multiculturalism Act. Whereas the federal law applies only to communications on the Internet or over the phone, Alberta's law goes further, covering "any statement, publication, notice, sign, symbol, emblem or other representation." That pretty much catches every form of expression, from smoke signals to semaphore flags to, in my case, publishing a magazine.

The law puts pretty broad limits on freedom of speech, and the drafters of the law knew it. But they had a sense of humour, which seems to be rare in the human rights business: Immediately after setting out the most all-encompassing ban on controversial opinions known to Canada, they stuck in a follow-up subsection, Section 3(2), which reads: "Nothing in this section shall be deemed to interfere with the free expression of opinion on any subject."

Section 3(2) doesn't *guarantee* freedom of expression – which is the first blush impression you might get upon scanning the wording. It doesn't say that Section 3(1) applies only insofar as it doesn't tread on Canadians' constitutionally protected freedom of expression. The important word is *deemed*. It means that nothing in Section 3(2) shall be *thought* of as interfering with the freedom of expression. A plain reading of Section 3(1) shows it to be an instrument of censorship. Section 3(2) spreads legal pixie dust in its wake, wishing that censorship away.

Although Alberta is often regarded as the freest Canadian province – it certainly thinks of itself that way, like a Texas of the north – it has been one of the most brutal in its enforcement of the thought crimes section of its human rights law.

Rev. Stephen Boissoin has first-hand experience. Reverend Boissoin isn't the sort of fellow who comes to mind when you think of a pastor. He's young, and he's a bodybuilder with biceps the size of hams. He has tattoos, remnants of a tough life on the streets that he left behind when he found religion – in his case, a socially conservative brand of Christianity.

In 2003, full of the zeal for his new life on the straight and narrow, Reverend Boissoin wrote a lengthy letter to the editor of his hometown paper, the *Red Deer Advocate*, in which he condemned homosexuality in no uncertain terms. It was a rough piece of work, rude even, and it was certainly provocative. One passage, for instance, declared: "Children as young as five and six years of age are being subjected to psychologically and physiologically damaging pro-homosexual literature and guidance in the public school system; all under the fraudulent guise of equal rights." But the newspaper deemed it fit for publication – and a torrent of reader responses as well. That's how debates about controversial subjects are supposed to work in a free society: we let ideas rise and fall according to the reception they get in the public square. But one Red Deerite didn't want a debate – he wanted the government to shut the other side up.

Darren Lund, a cranky anti-Christian activist teacher who'd already made a name for himself protesting against the proselytizing mission of Third World charity Operation Christmas Child, filed a complaint with the Alberta Human Rights and Citizenship Commission, claiming that Reverend Boissoin violated the province's thought crimes provisions.

In 2008, five grinding years later, the AHRCC issued its ruling: Reverend Boissoin's letter to the editor had broken the law. So said Lori Andreachuk, the one-woman human rights "panel" that issued the ruling. Andreachuk is a divorce lawyer by profession, with no expertise in constitutional freedoms.

As I noted earlier, human rights commissioners such as Andreachuk are limited-term political appointees. So when, in an extremely rare move, the provincial government intervened on behalf of Lund and against Reverend Boissoin, you can bet that Andreachuk was paying very close attention. In most cases, it is just the taxpayer-funded human rights commission's lawyers versus their target; this time, the prosecution was bolstered by a special lawyer sent by the provincial cabinet – the same people who would decide whether to reappoint Andreachuk to her patronage position.

The province's lawyer argued that "if people were allowed to simply hide behind the rubric of political and religious opinion, they would defeat the entire purpose of the human rights legislation." Given that free debate about religious and political matters has been fundamental to public life in Western society since the Enlightenment, that is a stunning and frightening statement. So, too, is the claim that "there is no such thing as 'discriminatory political and religious expression,' speech is either legitimate or it is discriminatory."

At any rate, Andreachuk did exactly what the province's lawyer petitioned her to do: she ruled that the feelings of sensitive bystanders "trumped the freedom of speech afforded in the Charter" and convicted Reverend Boissoin of illegal speech.

If that sounds outrageous, consider her punishments for Reverend Boissoin. "In this case," she wrote, "there is no specific individual who can be compensated as there is no direct victim who has come forward." What she meant, of course, was that *no one* was hurt by Reverend Boissoin's letter. The only human rights complainant was the town scold, a man who says he isn't gay and so couldn't possibly suffer any "hatred" due to the letter's publication. But in her ruling, Andreachuk described him as a human rights martyr anyway: "Lund, although not a direct victim, did expend considerable time and energy and suffered ridicule and harassment as a result of his complaint. The Panel finds therefore that he is entitled to some compensation."

Consider what went on here: A busybody with no connection to either Reverend Boissoin or the subject of his letter decides to go after the Reverend as part of what is essentially a freelance legal vendetta. Five years later, a government-appointed lawyer awards him a tax-free reward on the basis of "suffering" endured as a result of that same freely embarked-upon vendetta. In the end, Reverend Boissoin was ordered to pay Lund $5,000, and another $2,000 for Lund's expert witness.

But the money was the least of it. Andreachuk also ordered Reverend Boissoin to "cease publishing in newspapers, by email, on the radio, in public speeches, or on the Internet, in future, disparaging remarks about gays and homosexuals" – complete, blanket censorship, in other words.

If you're like me, you have nothing against gays. But we're talking here about a Christian pastor, a man whose whole life is oriented toward spreading the message of God as he understands it. Including his interpretation of the Bible's teachings on homosexuality. With her human rights judgment, Andreachuk made a mockery of that mission. Boissoin was not even permitted to communicate his opinions in sermons delivered in his church. If the state has no role in the bedrooms of our nation, why is it allowed in our churches and Bible classes?

Note, too, the elastic wording: Reverend Boissoin wasn't ordered to cease "hateful" comments, or "discriminatory" comments. He was ordered not to say anything "disparaging," a word that essentially means anything critical. Even members of the gay community itself routinely write critically about problems within their ranks. They can speak candidly. But not Reverend Boissoin – until the day he dies. There is no time limit on Andreachuk's gag order.

But it gets worse. Reverend Boissoin also is "prohibited from making disparaging remarks in the future about Dr. Lund or Dr. Lund's witnesses relating to their involvement in this complaint." For the rest of his life, Reverend Boissoin has been ordered not to criticize the man who, apparently for no other reason than his desire to shut up people who disagree with him, dragged him through half a decade of legal ordeal and, when all was said and done, took his money.

Like the commander of a Maoist re-education camp, Andreachuk ordered Reverend Boissoin to "provide Dr. Lund with a written apology for the article in the *Red Deer Advocate* that was the subject of this complaint." This was despite the fact that everyone involved with the case knew that any such apology would be insincere. Lund couldn't convince Reverend Boissoin that his views about gays were wrong. The human rights commission couldn't either. Even the full weight of the government of Alberta couldn't. All they could do was bully him into a coerced statement that Lund could hold up as a sort of human rights hunting trophy.

Reverend Boissoin was further ordered to "request [his] written apology for the contravention of the Act be published in the *Red Deer Advocate*." A government bureaucrat ordered a Canadian pastor, in essence, to publicly renounce his religious views as part of a state-enforced human-rights creed. What country are we in? North Korea? Iran?

Perhaps ironically, one of the groups that took a stand in favour of Reverend Boissoin's freedom of conscience was Egale, Canada's largest gay advocacy lobby. Originally, Lund had asked that Reverend Boissoin pay a fine to Egale. But the group, whose members still recall a past when the government used its censorship powers to block gay books and erotica, specifically refused to take it. They argued that a government that punishes a Christian for his views is no different and no better than one that punishes gays on the same basis.

As Gilles Marchildon, the executive director of Egale, wrote in a public letter, "while it is difficult to support Boissoin's right to spew his misguided and vitriolic thoughts, support his right, we must. If Boissoin was no longer able to share his views, then who might be next in also having their freedom of expression limited? Traditionally, the [gay] community's freedom has been repressed by society and its laws."

Moreover, he argued, allowing offensive speech – even "hate" speech, however that term might be defined – actually has some benefits for society: "It is far better that Boissoin expose his views than have them pushed underground. . . . His words may serve to increase public education."

Marchildon knows what any liberal activist who has studied history knows: that all progress comes from offending the status quo. From the fight to give women the right to vote, to the black civil rights movement of the 1960s, to the gay rights movement itself, free speech was the main tool for social change. It had to be: by definition, underdogs don't have money or political power, only the power of their ideas.

I am not suggesting that Reverend Boissoin's column put him in a league with Martin Luther King or Mahatma Gandhi. But once unleashed, censorship can bury social progressives as easily as it can bury Prairie pastors. And Marchildon was far-sighted enough to recognize that. It's too bad that Lund, the man who presumes to be offended on behalf of gay people such as Marchildon, isn't half as wise.

Some of the Canadians who've been charged under Section 13 of the Canadian Human Rights Act or its provincial equivalents, are genuinely bigoted individuals, which is why the HRCs have been able to enforce their censorship without much public reaction. But in recent years, HRCs have routinely targeted Canadians who are merely politically incorrect. One of the more surreal cases involves a comedian, someone whose *job* is to offend people.

Guy Earle is a small-time funny man – the kind of guy who works as an emcee at a local bar's open mic night in return for a fifty-dollar bar tab. He's not famous. And by his own admission, he's not always so funny – which likely explains why you've never heard of him. That's how the marketplace of ideas works, most of the time.

In May 2007, Earle hosted an evening of amateur comedy at Zesty's, a pub on Vancouver's seamy Commercial Drive. By all accounts, it was a rough night – a lot of kids coming up to the microphone who had no business being there. Earle numbed himself with vodka. Things got ever rockier when a woman named Lorna Pardy came in with her female date. The two girls got into the drinks pretty quickly, and before long were heckling Earle relentlessly from the front row. Apparently, however, the comedian's act wasn't so bad that it killed their romantic vibe. As the evening wore on, Pardy and her date started making out.

Comedy club hecklers may come across as buffoons to most of us. But comedians take them very seriously. Stand-up comedy – like any other public performance – works only when a comedian is in control of the room. An unchecked heckler challenges that control and can turn the crowd against the performer. Handled correctly, however, a heckler can also be an unexpected gift to a quick-witted comedian, providing him with someone to pick on – often with the support of the rest of the crowd.

Flipping a heckler to one's advantage is an art. The comedian must be sufficiently caustic to put the heckler in his or her place. But going too far with the insults can make a comedian appear cruel, insecure, or defensive.

On that fateful night, Earle erred in the latter direction. He let loose a tirade on Pardy and her date – who had progressed from heckling and necking to throwing two glasses of water on him. Flailing around for something to riff on, Earle targeted their lesbianism. A friend of the hecklers later paraphrased Earle's freakout as "You're fat and ugly, no wonder you're lesbians, you can't get a man." Was it funny? Since the episode wasn't recorded, I couldn't say. But I imagine it was raunchy: Earle warns audience members that his show is "triple-x-rated."

Some of the people in the audience reportedly booed Earle's tirade, presumably because they thought he was going overboard on the lesbian angle. But it's probably safe to assume that he would also have mocked a heterosexual couple that had heckled him in between bouts of necking. When you visit a comedy club – or at least when you decide to sit right up at the front and give the comedian a rough ride – you voluntarily assume the risk for being mocked. In the stand-up comedy business, turnaround is fair play, no matter what the heckler's race, sex, or sexual orientation is.

All in all, it was an awful night. Earle, Pardy, and her girlfriend probably all had an awful next morning too, given the reports of the drinking that went on. (According to the bar manager, Pardy and her girlfriend had been drinking for seven hours before she got into it with Earle.) But while Earle chalked it up to another night on the road in one of the toughest jobs anyone could choose, Pardy stomped off to the B.C. Human Rights Tribunal. In June 2008, the BCHRT confirmed that it was going to hear the matter, and set it down for a trial.

There is little doubt that Earle was offensive. He even admits to being an "asshole." But being an asshole isn't against the law. In the rough-and-tumble corners of the stand-up comedy trade, in fact, it's arguably a job requirement. Not all comics are as dirty as the late George Carlin or Andrew "Dice" Clay – or even Howard Stern. But there's no doubt that comedy is fundamentally transgressive. It's a political correctness–free zone, where people can laugh at life's contradictions and hypocrisies – and even laugh at themselves. It often involves saying things that you're "not supposed to" say. Even mainstream comedians and comedy shows, when scrutinized closely, would contravene some HRCs' hate speech laws.

Comedy is one of society's safety valves – something we use to discuss touchy subjects we aren't comfortable dealing with otherwise, including race, sex, religion, and sexual orientation. That's why humourless folks with a totalitarian outlook – intolerant religious zealots and hyper-tolerant human rights thought police alike – are so suspicious of comedy. They follow the dictum of Ayatollah Khomeini, who declared "Allah did not create man so that he could have fun. The aim of creation was for mankind to be put to the test through hardship and prayer. An Islamic regime must be serious in every field. There are no jokes in Islam. There is no humor in Islam. There is no fun in Islam. There can be no fun and joy in whatever is serious."

As George Orwell wrote, "Every joke is a tiny revolution." This subversive role of humour explains why it's so common for comedians to start off their routines with a bitter evisceration of . . . themselves. It's standard fare, for instance, to hear a Jewish comedian such as Jackie Mason poke fun at his culture's eccentricities. A comedy special by Chris Rock without the word *nigger* would be a very short evening. And even lesbian comedians – *especially* lesbian comedians – use their acts to examine the joy and pain associated with all-female romances. The jokes of Rosie O'Donnell or Ellen DeGeneres may be funnier than the put-downs of Guy Earle, but they poke fun at lesbians just the same. If that's not your thing, then don't go to the comedy club.

All of this rarefied discussion of the social meaning of comedy may seem unrelated to the two-bit rantings that went on at Zesty's. But it's not: if our society decides that stand-up routines can be censored in the name of diversity, then *all* comedians will feel the chill, and humour itself will wither.

Comparisons with the Soviet era – in regard to the Soviet instinct to suppress heterodox beliefs, if not in regard to their bloodthirsty methods – are inescapable. Joseph Stalin sent two hundred thousand people to the Gulag for making politically inappropriate jokes. Aleksandr Solzhenitsyn, the Nobel Prize–winning Russian writer, was sentenced to eight years of hard labour for writing a letter that poked fun at Stalin's moustache. The Nazis were just as wary: "humour has its limits," said Joseph Goebbels, Adolf Hitler's propaganda minister.

At root, that's why Earle is being taken to trial in Canada: It's now illegal to laugh about certain subjects. Canada's human rights commissions aren't just in the business of telling us how to run our businesses and our lives – they're now our official joke testers.

How could such a clearly unconstitutional law – a clearly un-*Canadian* law – continue to be abused this way? Why hasn't the Supreme Court struck Section 13 and its provincial counterparts down as an illegal violation of the Charter rights?

In fact, the Supreme Court did review Section 13, back in 1990, in a case called *Taylor.* John Taylor of Toronto, a prominent neo-Nazi leader, was the first person to be prosecuted under Section 13. In 1979, the CHRC charged him with hate speech and subsequently with contempt of court. In 1990, in the narrowest of decisions – four judges to three – the Supreme Court upheld the ruling against Taylor, saying that the hate speech law was permissible because "there is little danger that subjective opinion as to offensiveness will supplant the proper meaning of the section" – the "proper meaning" being that Section 13 should be used only against "ardent and extreme" hate.

The Supremes – or at least four of them – specified that the kind of language being targeted by Section 13 should be truly "evil," and that the law was "sufficiently precise to prevent the unacceptable chilling of expressive activity." Three judges objected – including Justice Beverley McLachlin, who has since gone on to become the Chief Justice of the Supreme Court.

The three justices' dissenting words in that 1990 case were prescient. In the nearly two decades since the court told Canadians not to worry about political abuses of the law, such abuses have continued to accumulate. No reasonable person would say that the ad-libbing of comedian Guy Earle, or the letter of socially conservative Rev. Stephen Boissoin, or my publication of the Danish cartoons, or Mark Steyn's well-researched, bestselling book about radical Islam were "evil." Yet all of these individuals – and hundreds more besides – have been prosecuted, chilled, or bullied by a law ostensibly designed for neo-Nazis and Holocaust deniers. Almost two decades after *Taylor*, the CHRC has a 100 per cent conviction rate in cases that go to trial under Section 13 – another troubling sign that the "evil" and the merely politically correct are being swept up by the same censorious legislation.

One of the reasons why the four judges in the *Taylor* majority thought it would be okay to leave such a blunt instrument in the hands of bureaucrats is that the HRCs aren't criminal courts, and they therefore can't punish their targets in the same way that a convicted criminal is punished. But even that turned out to be untrue. John Taylor was in his seventies when the case bearing his name was heard and sentenced to a year in jail for refusing to stop communicating his politically offensive theories. He served nine months. That punishment was technically for contempt of court, but it arose from his HRC prosecution. And a year in jail is much longer than many true criminals face, including many convicted for violent crimes.

And since *Taylor*, HRCs have developed a new form of punishment that even criminal courts aren't allowed to impose on criminal defendants: gross delays and huge costs. In another 1990 case called *Askov*, the Supreme Court ruled that criminals who don't get a speedy trial could go free – a ruling that caused thousands of accused criminals to walk away from the charges they faced – because prosecutors had been too slow to get them to trial. (These included Elijah Askov and three others who were charged with extortion in November of 1983 but were still awaiting trial in 1987.)

That's how our justice system treats people accused of true crimes: We are so scrupulous not to offend their constitutional rights, so careful not to make the process itself a punishment, that we let people accused of serious crimes walk free if the justice system doesn't play by the rules.

Compare that to the standards followed by HRCs. Reverend Boissoin's case took five years, and he hasn't even had his appeal yet. The most prominent Section 13 case, against alleged white supremacist Marc Lemire, is at five years and running. Fewer than 10 per cent of all Section 13 targets were able to afford the five- or six-figure price tag to engage a lawyer for the lengthy HRC process. Yet throughout, they were up against not only the CHRC's in-house legal team, paid for by taxpayers, but also, in most cases (such as Reverend Boissoin's and Lemire's), the legal resources of interveners.

In other words, the reasons that the Supreme Court cited in giving HRCs the benefit of the constitutional doubt – that they weren't as punitive as criminal courts, and that they could be expected to confine their investigations to genuinely "evil" hatemongers – have been debunked by events. Section 13 has become the worst of both worlds: a tool to beat political dissidents with police raids, five-year-long trials, arbitrary procedure, and, if it comes to it, jail time – but with none of the protections that we see fit to grant even to murderers and extortionists.

In the nearly twenty years since the law's legality was last tested, Canada's HRCs have shown that they can't be trusted with the awesome powers granted to them by Parliament. Fortunately, it is only a matter of time before another constitutional challenge to Section 13 gets to the Supreme Court. And this time, the result may be different than it was in 1990. That's because in recent years, the Supreme Court has taken a stronger stand on free expression – most notably in the above-described 2008 defamation case involving former Vancouver radio host Rafe Mair. As Justice Ian Binnie wrote, "We live in a free country where people have as much right to express outrageous and ridiculous opinions as moderate ones." Unfortunately, until the Supreme Court gets the chance to correct its 1990 error, that right will remain under threat.

Chapter 5

THE NEW BREED OF HUMAN RIGHTS ACTIVIST

Canada's human rights commissions have changed since they came into being in the 1960s and 1970s. They've gone from fighting for equal rights for individuals to fighting for special rights for groups. They've gone from being an informal "people's court" for disadvantaged minorities who are truly at risk to being a parallel legal system run by left-wing social engineers. As HRCs have lost their way, the kind of people who work for them have changed too.

A generation ago, the HRCs were championed by the same breed of bold civil rights crusaders who were fighting for equality all across North America. We didn't have world-famous orators such as Martin Luther King, Jr. But we did have our share of principled activists – men such as Alan Borovoy.

Borovoy was born in Canada in 1932. His lifelong love for civil liberties began at his bar mitzvah, in 1945, when his grandfather spoke to him tearfully about the tragedy that had befallen Europe's Jews in the Holocaust. Borovoy says he realized that the best way to protect anyone's rights was to protect everyone's rights. Before long, Borovoy was an activist for anyone he thought was on society's margins. In his twenties, he led the campaign to end discrimination against blacks in Nova Scotia's Africville ghetto. He organized rallies for Aboriginal peoples in downtown Toronto, pressing for such basics as running water. In 1968, he became general counsel to the Canadian Civil Liberties Association, a post he's held ever since.

Not surprisingly, Borovoy has noticed some changes in the fight for civil rights over the past four decades. Perhaps the biggest is this: while the abusers of civil rights in the 1960s and 1970s came from the right, today they're more likely to come from the left. In 1999, he even wrote a book about that transformation, called *The New Anti-Liberals* – a phrase chosen to prick the conscience of his former ideological allies.

"If we lose our freedoms in this country," Borovoy recently told a Toronto newspaper, "the job will be done to us not by malevolent autocrats seeking to do bad but by parochial bureaucrats seeking to do good." As a former labour union organizer, Borovoy remembers the days when agitating on the left meant being a downtrodden outsider. Now, the leftists are on the inside, abusing the same government power they once railed against.

More than anything, Borovoy disagrees with his former comrades-in-arms over the growth of government censorship in Canada. He, too, feels that racists should be hounded out of government offices – such as notorious anti-Semite Jim Keegstra, who was once the mayor of tiny Eckville, Alberta. But he argues that the marginalization of racists should be the result of public pressure, not hate speech laws such as Section 13 of the federal Human Rights Act.

"Go after them in the political arena. Raise hell about what they say. Force them to apologize," says Borovoy. "Distinguish between those who have standing and those who don't. I didn't think [Ernst] Zundel [an attention-seeking Holocaust denier who lived in Canada from 1958 to 2000] was worth the effort, but Keegstra was when he was a mayor and a teacher. But once he was decertified as a teacher and ousted as mayor, there was no point in prosecuting him, and he should have been allowed to wallow in the obscurity he so richly deserved."

Borovoy has been uncomfortable for a long time with the prosecution of fringe racists; he intervened on behalf of John Taylor and he's been railing against the law ever since. When the *Western Standard* magazine and I were charged with hate speech under Alberta's version of Section 13, Borovoy wrote that he couldn't believe what had become of his once-noble crusade for human rights. "Despite my considerable involvement in pressuring the Ontario government, many years ago, to create Canada's first human rights commission, I regret the attempt to use the law in this way," he wrote in a public letter.

"There should be no question of the right to publish the cartoons in question. Religious prophets no less than political leaders or even deities must be legally permissible targets of satire or even scorn. This is the essence of free speech in a democracy. No ideology – political, religious, or philosophical – can be immune. It would be wise, therefore, to remove those provisions of the Human Rights Act that could arguably sustain this complaint." But Borovoy is tilting at an organization that's become a full-fledged industry unto itself – a far cry from the shoestring citizens organizations he helped found in the 1960s.

There are still a few old school civil libertarians such as Borovoy around. But not many. He's from a different era, when civil rights activists were mainly volunteers, often putting themselves in genuine jeopardy of physical harm, especially in the deep South. To this day, Borovoy himself works on a small budget and has a tiny staff; his organization works almost exclusively through volunteer lawyers going to court on their own time to fight the hundreds of tiny incursions of the government – before they get bigger.

How different that is from today's human rights commissions. First off, the name is different: Borovoy doesn't use the term *human rights*. He sticks with the phrase *civil rights*, and he knows exactly what it means – fundamental individual freedoms, equality before the law, and natural justice. The phrase *human rights* in Canada has come to mean any desire, entitlement, or grievance dressed up as a right. And usually, that right is claimed by representatives of politically correct groups, not individual human beings.

It's instructive to compare Borovoy with one of Canada's current crop of activists. Richard Warman, a hyper-litigious Ottawa-based lawyer, loves complaining about human rights violations so much that he actually went to work for the Canadian Human Rights Commission from 2002 to 2004. He would investigate complaints by day and file his own complaints with the CHRC by night. He didn't investigate the same complaints that he'd filed; his colleagues at work did that. But he'd help them out, and they'd even let him poke around their work. It was pretty cozy.

Warman has been the complainant in all but one of the Section 13 hate speech hearings in the past six years. Given the federal Human Rights Commission's 100 per cent conviction rate on Section 13 cases, it goes without saying that Warman won them all – receiving awards of close to $50,000 in tax-free cash for his "pain and suffering." How can one man file dozens of complaints? Is there some worldwide conspiracy to discriminate against him? Or is he just ridiculously sensitive?

Like Borovoy, Warman is a lifelong activist. He unsuccessfully ran for election four times for the Green Party but soon realized that a radical such as he could achieve more through lawfare than through politics. But where Borovoy would fight against real discrimination – blacks not allowed in white restaurants; Indian reserves with Third World living conditions – Warman chose as his mission the elimination of bad words. Every single complaint he has filed has been a Section 13 speech case.

Borovoy's place was on the streets, with the disenfranchised. Warman's place is in front of his computer, surfing Internet chat rooms under various nicknames. While he was a CHRC investigator, he would become a member of American neo-Nazi websites. He would write bigoted comments on the Internet – disparaging Jews, blacks, gays, even fat people. He would engage other online neo-Nazis in conversation. And whenever he encountered other Canadians doing the same thing, he would try to get them to reveal their identity to him – and then he'd slap them with a personal Section 13 human rights complaint.

Unlike police, however, human rights commissioners don't have the right to break the law (in this case, Section 13 of the Canadian Human Rights Act) in order to enforce it. And for good reasons. When police forces send someone undercover, there are rules about what they can and can't do, what laws they can bend and what laws they can't. And the whole thing is supervised carefully by other police, to make sure the undercover agent doesn't lose perspective or get in too deep. The CHRC does not have these kinds of safeguards, so Warman's extracurricular adventures to generate human rights complaints were unfettered by the sorts of checks and balances we normally apply to government workers with investigatory powers.

But there's a deeper difference, as well: undercover cops are legally permitted to entrap someone through simulated bad behaviour – they might pose as a prostitute to entrap a john, for instance; or they might pose as a drug buyer to catch a drug dealer. But CHRC investigators don't have that right. Any CHRC investigator who spreads hate on the Web as part of an effort to entrap neo-Nazis is liable under Section 13 and even under the hate speech provisions of the Canadian Criminal Code. So what is a $25-million-a-year human rights organization doing paying someone to go online to foment racial discord? How does adding to the bigotry on the Internet make the world a less bigoted place?

Warman praised neo-Nazis online, called for unity among various neo-Nazi splinter groups, and even signed off one of his online comments with Nazi shorthand for "heil Hitler." He denounced what he said was Jewish control of government and the media; he even attacked a Jewish youth group, saying its real "goal is to tear people down." He called for support of a convicted white supremacist terrorist in the United States, he wrote favourably about a racist 1981 book called *White Man's Bible*, and he complained that some neo-Nazi activists weren't white enough. Warman called for the establishment of an all-white city called "Whiteville"; he said that "white cops" should "stand by their race." He called the federal government's cabinet ministers "scum" because they were too pro-Jewish. And he denounced gays as "sexual deviants" who are a "cancer" on society.

That's pretty vile stuff; and Warman made literally hundreds of such online posts over the course of several years. It's unthinkable that a civil rights activist of the 1960s generation would ever engage in such bigotry himself. Borovoy, as I've noted, is old school, a relic of an earlier, more idealistic age. He looks at civil rights as a calling, a lifelong commitment to high ideals, a personal sacrifice for the betterment of all humanity. He would never call gays or Jews – or anyone, even someone he bitterly disagreed with – a "cancer" or "scum." He wouldn't lodge a complaint and ask to personally pocket a bounty. Warman, however, willingly signed up as a member of these U.S. neo-Nazi organizations, then demanded – and received – awards of tens of thousands of dollars for the "pain and suffering" he experienced from the bigots he tangled with.

Today's HRCs are political weapons, whereby radical activists can earn a secure, tax-funded livelihood while pursuing their political agendas. Warman even gave his agenda a name: "Maximum Disruption." That's the title of a speech Warman gave to a violent street gang called Anti-Racist Action, in which he told them how he likes to deal with his enemies.

> I've come to the conclusion that I can be most effective by using what I like to describe as a "maximum disruption" approach . . . I'll look at all of the potential targets and file complaints against them starting on a "worst offender" basis, although sometimes if I just find people to be particularly annoying this may move them up the list a bit.
>
> The "maximum disruption" part comes in because wherever I think it will be most helpful, or even if I just feel it will be the most fun, I strongly believe in hitting [them] on as many of these fronts as possible either at the same time or one after the other. I say this because it keeps them off-balance and forces them to respond to things that focus their energies on defending themselves.

Warman practises what he preaches. In addition to filing dozens of complaints with the federal HRC, he has filed or threatened dozens of defamation lawsuits against almost anyone who criticizes him – including many of the people he also targets at the HRC.

One of Warman's more colourful targets is David Icke, a former soccer player from Britain who, one day, stunned his fans by announcing his revelation that the world is controlled by reptilian humanoids from outer space who are linked to the tract *The Protocols of the Elders of Zion*, an anti-Semitic hoax. Icke's ideas are unusual, to say the least, but there's not a harmful bone in his body. Warman, though, is convinced that this conspiracy theorist is a menace to human rights.

When Icke came to Canada to promote a book outlining his theories, Warman went into Maximum Disruption mode, calling up media outlets to try to get them to cancel interviews with him. It didn't work very well – as usual, attempts to censor someone only stir up more interest in what they're saying. So Warman came up with a new plan: send a pack of youths to a bookstore where Icke was speaking, and have them throw a pie at him, to "take the piss out of him" and "humiliate" him in front of his fans.

Icke had said that Warman was one of the aliens controlling the world. But instead of laughing it off, Warman sued him for defamation – and even threatened to sue Canadian libraries that stocked Icke's strange books. Faced with unaffordable legal fees, the Toronto Public Library caved in, pulling Icke's books off the shelves. Faced with similar threats, the province of British Columbia, to its credit, actually passed a special law protecting libraries from defamation lawsuits.

Richard Warman may be Canada's most prolific human rights complainer, but the human rights activist with the biggest public profile would have to be Barbara Hall, the chief commissioner of the Ontario Human Rights Commission.

Hall, who was turfed by voters as Toronto's mayor in 1997, has had a political comeback as a bureaucratic appointee. She has a vision for the OHRC – a vision that includes thousands more complaints being filed each year, and unlimited awards for "pain and suffering" being paid out. Thanks in part to her agitation, Ontario recently changed its human rights law: citizens can now take their complaints directly to a human rights hearing, skipping the vetting process that once weeded out obviously meritless complaints. At the same time, OHRC officials no longer just prosecute complaints, they drum them up.

Hall has big plans. But to make them happen, she needs to foment a lot more misery. "I would say that for a province as large and as diverse as Ontario, to have 2,500 formal complaints a year, that that's a very low level," she told the *National Post*. The number of complaints "may have to spike." In other words, as Hall sees it, Ontarians are too satisfied with their lives. The province's race and gender relations are excessively harmonious. If Hall and her friends are going to keep their jobs – and their budgets – Ontarians are going to have to do a lot more griping about each other.

Unlike the laws of the federal Human Rights Commission, the AHRCC, and the BCHRT, Ontario's human rights law doesn't contain a hate speech provision that covers the media – so in early 2008, when she received a complaint against *Maclean's* magazine for publishing Mark Steyn's 2006 article on the threat posed by radical Islam, Hall simply couldn't stretch her legislative mandate to cover this juicy censorship opportunity.

But Hall couldn't resist the opportunity to tell Ontarians how she would have decided this case – if only the law had given her the censorship power she craved. Her press release on the subject is a truly creepy document, and is worth excerpting at length:

> While freedom of expression must be recognized as a cornerstone of a functioning democracy, the Commission has serious concerns about the content of a number of articles concerning Muslims that have been published by *Maclean's* magazine and other media outlets. . . . While we all recognize and promote the inherent value of freedom of expression, it should also be possible to challenge any institution that contributes to the dissemination of destructive, xenophobic opinions. . . .
>
> Although the Commission has decided that there is no basis in the Code to take these complaints forward, it has a broader duty to express its opinion regarding issues that are brought to its attention which have implications from a human rights perspective. Islamophobic attitudes are becoming more prevalent in society and Muslims are increasingly the target of intolerance, including an unwillingness to consider accommodating some of their religious beliefs and practices. Unfortunately, the *Maclean's* article, and others like it, are examples of this.
>
> The Commission supports freedom of thought, belief, opinion and expression, as enshrined in the Canadian Charter of Rights and Freedoms. [But] with rights come responsibilities. . . . In Canada, the right to freedom of expression is not absolute, nor should it be. . . . The different approaches in various human rights statutes across Canada can send a confusing message and give rise to inconsistencies, depending on where a complaint is filed. . . . Clearly more debate on this

> issue is required in Canada. A comprehensive approach to the issue should be one of the goals.

Translation: Hall is upset that Ontario's human rights statute doesn't permit her to act as censor-at-large, and she wants the province to adopt a more "comprehensive approach" that would grant her the same powers wielded by human rights thought police in other jurisdictions.

Equally frightening is Hall's idea that "with rights come responsibilities" – a superficially earnest-sounding phrase that is in fact quite Orwellian. Think about it: What good is a "right" to free speech if you have a government-enforced "responsibility" to use that right in a government-enforced manner? The Soviet Union, too, safeguarded the right of "free speech" – so long as citizens abided by their "responsibility" to avoid counterrevolutionary topics.

When she was mayor, Barbara Hall had to spend a lot of her time worrying about such banal issues as garbage collection and bus routes – always with the voters' judgment hanging over her head. As an unelected human rights official, she has carte blanche to live out her nanny state dreams. And best of all – no matter how radical her pronouncements – no one can vote her out of office.

There are a lot of characters such as Warman and Hall running around Canada's HRCs. Take a lawyer at Alberta's HRC named Arman Chak.

Chak comes from an ambitious family; his brother, Farhan Chak, briefly ran as a candidate for the federal Liberal Party, until party officials discovered that he had padded his resumé

– and that he was a raging Jew-hater who had once shot up an Edmonton nightclub. Farhan would probably do better back in the lawless mountain ranges of Pakistan; here in Canada, Arman is the more successful brother. He ran for public office too – in an Alberta-wide election among lawyers to choose who would govern the law society. Arman came in dead last.

Arman may be unpopular among his fellow lawyers, but he is a lawyer nonetheless – and helped his brother send out dozens of lawsuit threats to newspapers and even websites that reported Farhan's embarrassing ouster from the Liberal Party. But Arman Chak isn't just about family solidarity. He's about religious solidarity, and in particular the unity of the Muslim world, or *ummah*. Chak is a Muslim supremacist, and believes that the world is divided into two halves: dar al Islam, or the "house of Islam"; and dar al Harb, the "house of war" – a category that includes all non-Muslims

Chak and his brother were regular writers to a radical website called Pakistan Link. There, they would rail against Muslims who took a moderate approach to politics. Arman Chak argued, for example, that the country of Bangladesh had no right to exist – it properly belonged to Pakistan, and it was only because of the interference of a non-Muslim country, India, that Bangladesh and Pakistan were broken up, "a precedent the world wishes to forget." Chak also wrote longingly about "the fundamentals of an Islamic State and its Muslim identity"; the fact that Bangladesh dared to be friendly with the non-Muslim state of India was "one of the worst examples of the dis-unification of the Muslim ummah in contemporary history." He argues that Bangladesh is an illegal breakaway country – just as "illegal" as Israel, which Chak says has "no right" to exist.

That's not accurate, of course. The Jewish state has the rare distinction of having actually been created by a vote of the United Nations. Notwithstanding such logical glitches, Muslim supremacists who daydream about one big Muslim superstate aren't breaking any laws. When they whip up hostility online against India, Bangladesh, and Israel, that shouldn't be against the law, either (though given the broad reach of Section 13, it probably is). In a nation that honoured free speech, Chak and his brother would be free to rant all they like, as long as they lay off shooting up night clubs.

Arman Chak has also got every right to be an amateur film-maker, producing such indy gems as *Qiyamat* – named after the Muslim word for the Apocalypse. Each to his own. But is it appropriate for such a radical to be a staff lawyer at the Alberta Human Rights Commission, whose mandate is to improve inter-ethnic relations in Alberta? Is it possible for someone who whips up racial and religious hostility on the Web in his spare time to be a harmony-building, tolerant multiculturalist from 9 to 5?

Consider if the shoe were on the other foot: Imagine the likelihood that the HRC would hire a white staff lawyer who spends his evenings writing his honestly believed anti-Semitic, anti-black, and anti-gay comments on the Internet.

What happens when someone from India, Bangladesh, or Israel – three countries Chak apparently despises – presents him- or herself to the HRC with a complaint? Will Chak chuck it? Or – less hypothetically – what happens when a fellow Pakistani immigrant files a complaint with the HRC against an Alberta magazine for publishing Danish cartoons of Mohammed?

Is the fact that Syed Soharwardy's absurd complaint against me and the *Western Standard* magazine was accepted and prosecuted vigorously by the AHRCC related in any way to his ideological kinship with Chak? In a real court, even the appearance of such a conflict of interest would be a huge, flashing red light.

And then there's Sandy Kozak, an investigator with the CHRC. She was assigned the case of *Maclean's* magazine. Kozak specializes in censorship: she was also the CHRC officer who launched a completely futile fifteen-month investigation of a small Toronto magazine called *Catholic Insight* because that magazine promoted the Vatican's view on gay marriage.

What are Kozak's credentials for being on the CHRC's political vice squad? On the plus side, Kozak has actually worked for a real police force, in Carleton Place, Ontario. She went through the academy, knows how to use walkie-talkies, and even carried a gun. On top of that, she was the first female cop on the force. And on the minus side? Just one item – but it's a biggie: Kozak was drummed out of the Carleton Place Municipal Police Service force for corruption. She had her badge and her gun stripped from her, then struck a deal with her employers to go quietly rather than face a full-blown trial.

When Kozak was still carrying a badge, she struck up a romantic relationship with Ryan Jones – a criminal under investigation by the very same Carleton Place police force. Now Jones wasn't an ex-con trying to get his life back together after paying his debt to society. No, he was still on the loose, and Kozak's fellow officers were doing everything they could to bust him.

When the police department found out about the relationship, they asked Kozak to choose: her duty to the law, or her affections for a criminal. When she refused to make a decision, the Carleton Place police department duly threw out their first female officer, a five-year veteran of the force.

Jones was no murderer. He was wanted for assault and possession of stolen property. Oh, and when he and Kozak began dating, he was under investigation for harassment. But Kozak has "helped straighten me out," he quipped to reporters – as he and Kozak engaged in a public display of affection on the courthouse steps.

The ex-cop was defiant, telling reporters she would be "looking at other policing opportunities. It's what I want to do and I'm not going to let this get in my way." But no self-respecting police force in North America would hire a rogue cop fired from the force for associating with a criminal. A cop not only has to respect the law, she must be seen to respect the law as well.

But at CHRC, they were delighted to hire a defrocked, corrupt cop. Kozak behaviour didn't conflict with the CHRC's code of ethics – because the CHRC quite literally doesn't have a code of ethics.

Five years ago, the CHRC underwent an audit of its management practices. The sixty-seven-page final report, stamped "private and confidential" on every page, measured everything from financial accounting systems to risk management to how the CHRC does its planning. It was an exhaustive inspection of CHRC operations.

The CHRC got a failing grade. Not a single one of the thirty-three areas examined by the auditors received a mark of "best practice" or even "advanced practice." Many of the basic management techniques were simply non-existent. The CHRC is a two-hundred-person, $25-million-a-year boondoggle.

But the most striking finding of the audit was that "the Commission does not have in place a formal ethics framework and does not have a formal structure and designated champion for ethics." As Richard Warman's involvement with the CHRC shows, anything goes. That's bad news for taxpayers, that's bad news for citizens targeted by the CHRC, and that's bad news for Canadians concerned about obvious ethical lapses. But it's good news for disgraced cops looking for work. That's the new breed of human rights activists in Canada. They're not fit to shine Borovoy's shoes.

Chapter 6

EASY TARGETS: HUMAN RIGHTS TRIBUNALS AND LAWFARE

As I've explained in previous chapters, the term *human rights commission* is increasingly becoming a misnomer: many of the cases that HRCs now adjudicate have nothing to do with human rights.

As Canada's HRCs started getting a reputation for eroding the right to freedom of speech and religion, they started attracting the attention of radical Muslim activists, who have long sought to squelch criticism of their ideology. It's part of an international strategy by Muslim radicals to use liberal, Western laws to make lawfare a form of what I call "soft jihad."

I was the first target of Islamic lawfare at Canada's HRCs. In February 2006, the *Western Standard* magazine, of which I was then publisher, reprinted the Danish cartoons of Mohammed as a news item, to show our readers what all the fuss was about. (At the time, the images had caused deadly riots around the world.) Immediately, both the magazine and I were hit with a human rights complaint.

The next target of this kind of censorship was *Maclean's* magazine, which, in late 2006, published an excerpt from Mark Steyn's bestselling book about Muslim demographics.

And in the boldest example yet, in May 2008, Atlantic Canada's largest newspaper, the Halifax *Chronicle-Herald*, was hit with a human rights complaint after its award-winning political cartoonist, Bruce MacKinnon, depicted a local Muslim radical in a full burka – which is, in fact, how she dresses. The fact that the Halifax police were called in to perform their own investigation makes that case especially troubling. Their involvement signified the politicization of the constabulary in the name of political correctness, a violation of the separation of mosque and state, and a lurch away from Canadian values.

None of the above-described HRC targets actually discriminated against anyone. They were media organizations publishing news and opinion. None of the complainants were denied the right to subscribe to the newspaper or magazine based on their race; none were denied a job based on their religion. These complainants just didn't like what they read, so they sued in the only forum that wouldn't kick them out or make them ante up for legal costs.

There's something very perverse at work here: Based on their illiberal dogmas, you'd think these complainants would be on the other side of a human rights hearing, being made to answer for their intolerance of "infidels." How did our human rights tribunals become such easy targets for these practitioners of soft jihad?

The case against me and the *Western Standard* magazine was brought by a Calgary imam named Syed Soharwardy, a Pakistani-born, madrassah-trained preacher popular on the

Saudi lecture circuit who is the president of the Islamic Supreme Council of Canada. Soharwardy's allies in the Edmonton Council of Muslim Communities soon piled on with an identical complaint. (I'll be talking about that experience in more detail later.)

Syed Soharwardy's hand-scrawled complaint to the Alberta HRC is remarkable: it cites the Koran as its legal basis, and Soharwardy himself claims standing because he is a "direct descendant" of Mohammed. That may sound nuts, but it's as close to normal as Soharwardy gets. He has publicly called for the replacement of Canada's secular government with sharia law. In other words, he wants to replace our constitution with the Koran – just like in Saudi Arabia. As he wrote in the *Calgary Herald*, "these universal, divine laws are for all people of all countries for all times." If he had his way, Canadians would be living in a Muslim theocracy.

Soharwardy is more than a big talker about sharia law. He was one of the Muslim leaders who actually tried to start a Muslim court system in Canada to replace our secular judiciary, especially in the field of divorce law. That's not just a threat to the separation of religion and state, it's a shot at the Canadian belief in the equality of men and women. In Soharwardy's utopia, girls get only half the inheritance that boys do and it takes the testimony of two women to equal that of one man in court. His world view is quite literally medieval.

Soharwardy's opinions about women aren't the only un-Canadian thing about him. He's full of venom toward other religions, from Jews to Christians to rival Muslim sects. Soharwardy claims that Israel's treatment of Palestinians is "worse than the Holocaust of World War II." Soharwardy wasn't quite clear about how, exactly, a dispute over territory in the Middle East that has claimed several thousand lives could be worse than Hitler's slaughter of six million Jews. But for this imam, such details are beside the point. The purpose of his statement was to take the lowest point of Jewish history and throw it mockingly in the face of Canadian Jews. It was a grotesque thing to say – the kind of thing that might get white racists in Canada charged with a Section 13 hate crime if they dared broach the subject.

Soharwardy doesn't spare Christians either – even though countries whose populations are mostly Christian (whether secular or practising) are spending billions of dollars helping Muslims on the other side of the world. After the 2004 tsunamis killed more than two hundred thousand people, most of them Indonesian Muslims, Western governments and charities took the lead in sending relief – an effort spearheaded by the Australian and U.S. navies. Where most people saw interfaith solidarity, Soharwardy saw a modern-day crusade. He sent out a bizarre news release accusing Western aid agencies of kidnapping Muslim children in Indonesia to forcibly convert them to Christianity. It was a baseless, vile lie – but no worse than his slur that the Jews were the new Nazis.

Even fellow Muslims don't escape Soharwardy's wrath if they happen to be from a sect he doesn't like. When Prime Minister Stephen Harper attended the opening of Canada's largest mosque in the summer of 2008, Soharwardy called media across the country to denounce the mosque as counterfeit – because it belonged to the Ahmadiyya sect of Islam, a peaceful minority that itself is picked on in the Muslim world. (In Soharwardy's homeland of Pakistan, anti-Ahmadiyya bigotry is written right in to the constitution.)

Anti-Jewish, anti-Christian, and anti-Ahmadiyya – Soharwardy has all the bases covered. And, just in case you missed the point,

Soharwardy's own website publishes an editorial written by Yusuf al-Qaradawi, a senior adviser to The Muslim Brotherhood, the spiritual antecedent to Hamas and al Qaeda. Al-Qaradawi is a supporter of suicide bombings in Israel. He is also a Holocaust denier. He approved when the Taliban blew up ancient statues of Buddha in 2001. One of his nuttiest rulings was a fatwa against the Japanese computer game Pokemon because, he claimed, the fictional characters squeaked "I am a Jew" and "Become a Jew" in Japanese. He's so rabid in his opinions that he's banned from even visiting Britain and the United States. And this is the man Soharwardy looks up to as an authority worthy of publishing on his website.

It gets worse: Soharwardy, that great champion of human rights, has himself been the subject of two human rights complaints filed by women in his congregation who allege that he has mistreated and harassed them. Within months of filing those complaints, one of the three women was beaten to the point of hospitalization in a home invasion and another had her house torched. Soharwardy has not been charged in either crime. But according to police, as the assaulted woman was being beaten, her assailant told her to stop criticizing Soharwardy's mosque. It's passing strange that such a man, with such a troubled mosque, could bend a Canadian human rights commission to his will for so long.

One of Soharwardy's fellow Islamists, Mohamed Elmasry, has given his own personal project a similarly grandiose name as Soharwardy's: The Canadian Islamic Congress. Elmasry, an engineering professor at the University of Waterloo in Ontario, is the complainant behind the three human rights lawsuits against *Maclean's* magazine; CIC filed identical complaints with the OHRC, BCHRT, and CHRC. But even the quickest review of Elmasry's own track record should make one wonder: Why hasn't he been the subject of a human rights complaint himself?

Elmasry first came to national prominence in 2004, when he appeared on the *Michael Coren Show,* a television program broadcast out of CTS studios in Burlington, Ontario, in a debate about the Middle East. On live TV, Elmasry argued that it was legitimate for terrorists to kill any Jewish adult in Israel. Coren, the host, was flabbergasted, and thought Elmasry had misspoken. He asked his guest to clarify his remarks, and clarify he did: He meant every word he said. Like Soharwardy, Elmasry was simply following the fatwa of al-Qaradawi and the Muslim Brotherhood. What was so surprising about that?

Elmasry didn't think he'd done anything wrong, but his employer was horrendously embarrassed. The university issued a press release condemning Elmasry's comments as "abhorrent" and "unacceptable." And Elmasry himself was forced to disavow his own clearly expressed comments. But he's kept at his radical activism ever since.

Surfing through Elmasry's official website feels like a visiting a Holocaust museum – except that the anti-Semitism is expressed in English and Arabic, not German. Elmasry's CIC heartily endorses Iranian President Mahmoud Ahmadinejad, who seeks to annihilate Israel, and his military nuclear program. Exterminationist terrorist groups such as Hamas are regularly defended as legitimate. Even non-Muslim anti-Semites have their work published on the CIC website, which has been known to borrow from the neo-Nazi publication *National Vanguard.*

Many modern anti-Semites disguise their hatred of Jews by talking euphemistically about "Zionists." Not Elmasry. He says what he means: The Jews control the media, the Jews control the business world, and the Jews control the government. Is this a man who should be taken seriously when he complains that *Maclean's* magazine has "violated his human rights"? Does Elmasry even know what those words mean?

Out east, Elmasry's Maritime equivalent is Ziaullah Khan, the boss of a Halifax mosque called the Centre for Islamic Development. Khan is a bit of a movie star in his own right, having uploaded various of his sermons to the Internet. They're a good way to get a measure of the man who filed a human rights complaint against his local newspaper, the Halifax *Chronicle-Herald*.

One of Khan's video rants was about Aqsa Parvez, a Muslim teenager in Toronto whose father and brother have been charged with murdering her in 2007, allegedly as part of an "honour killing." Such killings are frighteningly common in the Muslim world, where men sometimes kill women who "dishonour" their family through a premarital sexual indiscretion or some other gesture of rebellion against their family's wishes. In Parvez's case, that source of dishonour allegedly was that she didn't want to wear a hijab to cover her head. It was a shocking murder that reminded people of the gulf between radical Islam and Canadian values, especially when it came to women's rights.

Ziaullah Khan's sermon about Parvez was laced with righteous fury. But his fury wasn't directed at Parvez's father and brother, nor a radicalized strain within Islam that treats women as chattels. No, his rage was aimed at the media, for daring to report on this crime. He called reporters the "hatemongers" in the story.

That's the man who lodged the complaint with the Nova Scotia Human Rights Commission when the *Chronicle-Herald* printed an editorial cartoon featuring a local Muslim radical dressed in a full, head-to-toe, Saudi-style burka.

The woman depicted was Cheryfa MacAulay Jamal. As her middle name suggests, she's a Christian convert to Islam. And like many converts, she goes a little overboard to prove her bona fides: Jamal doesn't leave the house without covering herself completely, except for a little slit through which her blue eyes and 1980s-style wire-rim glasses can be seen.

Jamal caught the interest of the *Chronicle-Herald*'s cartoonist when her husband, Qayyum Abdul Jamal, was arrested in a 2006 anti-terrorism raid. Qayyum was eventually released, and Cheryfa's angry reply was a perfect blend of militant Islam and Western materialist greed: "I want millions," she said, demanding compensation for her husband's arrest. That demand was the subject of the *Chronicle-Herald*'s cartoon.

The Jamal family didn't write a letter to the editor. They didn't ask for a meeting with the paper's editorial board. Neither did Khan. They didn't do what generations of Haligonians who have disagreed with their local media have done in the past. They couldn't sue the newspaper for defamation, for there was nothing defamatory about the cartoon; the paper could simply claim truth and fair comment. Instead, Khan followed the successful precedents of Soharwardy and Elmasry: He called the bureaucrats at the Nova Scotia Human Rights Commission, charging the *Chronicle-Herald* with discrimination. And they accepted the complaint and ran with it.

What's different about his case is that the *Chronicle-Herald* said they first heard of Khan's complaint not from the complainant, nor from the HRC, but from the police, who were asked to investigate. No matter what happens to Khan's HRC complaint, he's already won a huge victory. A radical imam managed to convince a secular Canadian police force to call up a newspaper to pass on a complaint about an editorial cartoon.

It's unthinkable that the Halifax police would have blurred the line between religion and state for any other group. The idea of a police officer walking into a Blockbuster and giving the manager a lecture about, say, *The Da Vinci Code* at the behest of a local Catholic priest is too ridiculous even to contemplate. Such an inappropriate intervention – such an obvious act of intimidation – would be national news were it performed at the direction of a Christian church. But in the name of political correctness, Ziaullah Khan – an endorser of the subjugation of women – can unleash not just the pretend police at the local human rights commission but also the real police against what he calls Islam's enemies.

What's going on here? With the exception of a handful of Muslim radicals, such as Arman Chak, Canada's HRCs are generally the preserve of middle-aged white folk. It says a lot about how thoroughly our society has distorted the concept of human rights over the years that leftist, feminist bureaucrats could unwittingly become the allies of angry men with fascist politics and medieval ideas about women's place in society.

Equally shocking is that a taxpayer-funded secular institution created to further the goal of multiculturalism and tolerance could be co-opted by Soharwardy, Elmasry, and Khan to prosecute what are essentially blasphemy suits against radical Islam's critics and satirists. How did we let Muslim radicals outsource their soft jihad to the Canadian government?

The hijacking of Canadian law to promote radical Islam is actually part of an international strategy proposed by the Organization of the Islamic Conference (OIC), an umbrella group representing the world's fifty-seven Muslim nations. In March 2008, the OIC met in Dakar, Senegal, with the express purpose of creating a "legal instrument" to block criticism of Islam. "I don't think freedom of expression should mean freedom from blasphemy," said Senegalese President Abdoulaye Wade, who chaired the meeting. "There can be no freedom without limits."

Taken to the extreme, such a carve-out from the right to free speech would effectively prohibit proselytizing on behalf of any faith except Islam. For example, Muslims believe that the Catholic trinity represents a form of polytheism, and thus amounts to blasphemy. Hinduism is verboten for the same reason. In fact, any faith that rejects Mohammed as its true prophet and the Koran as the word of God is, by definition, blaspheming against Islam.

Ekmeleddin İhsanoğlu, the secretary-general of the OIC, hit the same theme – but cleverly did so using the Western-friendly lexicon of human rights. Muslims, he said, "are being targeted by a campaign of defamation, denigration, stereotyping, intolerance and discrimination." Naturally, this could not be permitted to continue. Where Wade was speaking about blasphemy – making it illegal to criticize the religion of Islam itself – İhsanoğlu was talking about protecting Muslims from political criticism. Taken together, they amount to a blanket ban on any speech that the Mohamed Elmasrys and Syed Soharwardys of the world might find objectionable.

The OIC points out that, even in the West, ideologically driven censorship is hardly unknown: There are certain ideologies and beliefs that are legally protected from criticism. In some European countries, for instance, it's against the law to foment Nazism, or deny the Holocaust. Canada and European nations have laws against hate speech. The fact that these laws have historically been used to protect Jews isn't a problem for the OIC. Just the opposite: the group insists that Muslims merely want "equal treatment" with their religious rivals.

It's not equal treatment, of course. Judaism itself is not legally immune from criticism, nor is Israel, Zionism, or other topics connected to Judaism. But it must be conceded that there is a seed of truth to the Islamists' complaint: many Western nations have rendered certain subjects beyond the pale of debate. And now that we've opened the door of ideological censorship, other groups are predictably agitating for their pet causes to be added to the class of off-limits topics. And what excuse do we have for saying no? The example shows how the seed of censorship, once planted, always keeps growing.

In recent years, the OIC has started promoting a treaty to "combat the defamation of Islam," a document that could soon become part of the big vat of international law that slowly seeps into the laws of Western countries through the United Nations. In July 2008, the international ruckus caused by Canada's censorship in the name of human rights led to an invitation to me by the bi-partisan U.S. Congressional Human Rights Caucus. I was asked to come to Washington, D.C., as an expert witness about the threat posed by radical Islam using Western legal mechanisms as weapons. That's where I met Sandra Bunn-Livingstone, a lawyer for the U.S. State Department who was her country's point-woman on the Islamic defamation file. In analyzing the OIC's campaign, she compared the message contained in the group's official English-language statements and their rhetoric in Arabic. According to an Arabic linguist whom Bunn-Livingstone consulted, the word the OIC uses to describe "defamation of Islam" did not exist in Arabic before their political campaign – it was made up. The word that the OIC leaders use when speaking among themselves, on the other hand, is a traditional term that has no connection to *defamation.* It means blasphemy.

That's not just language trivia. It shows that the OIC's campaign against Western criticism is a fake. It's being sold to the West in non-threatening terms – twisting Western legal phrases such as *defamation* (which is illegal under secular law, after all, so what's the harm in banning it?) just enough to cover the true intentions. But when the Western media are gone, and the conversation reverts back to Arabic, it's all about the sharia concept of blasphemy.

One of George W. Bush's more persuasive rationales for fighting terrorism in Iraq and Afghanistan was that it took the battle to the bad guys – overseas, away from America itself. The OIC is doing exactly the same thing, but in reverse. By taking the battle over religious freedom and the right to dissent to the West – to the UN, to the European Union, to courts in Canada – radical Islam is pushing attention away from the Arab world's own abominable record when it comes to the treatment of religious minorities.

It's a good strategy – keep the West on the defensive, use the West's legal systems, and prey on the West's post-colonial guilt and cultural self-doubt. With all the talk about Islamophobia, there's not a lot of time left to talk about the persecution of Christians or apostate Muslims in Muslim countries. And Saudi Arabia, the driving force behind the OIC, likes that just fine.

The plan is going well. In recent years, the OIC even managed to get the United Nations Human Rights Council to modify its application of the UN's Universal Declaration of Human Rights so as to limit criticism of Islam. Indeed, thanks to bloc voting by Islamic nations and their autocratic allies, criticizing human rights abuses perpetrated in the name of sharia is now entirely taboo at the council.

Even more incredible is that the UN's Special Rapporteur on Freedom of Expression has now been turned into an agent of censorship. In early 2008, a coalition of Islamic states rammed through a UN resolution requiring the rapporteur to detail any free speech "abuse" against religion. A UN official whose job was once to protect freedom of speech will now be mandated to snitch on real civil rights activists who dare point out, for instance, that sharia laws are being used to justify medieval punishments against gays, infidels, and "fornicators" in hardline Islamic nations.

That will dovetail nicely with the OIC's own "observatory" project – their euphemism for spying on every conference, speech, or publication in the West that criticizes Islam, and thus is in need of a little lawfare.

In June 2008, the government of Pakistan – not exactly a beacon of freedom – sent a delegation to ask Europeans to curtail freedom of expression so as to "prevent offensive incidents" such as the dissemination of the 2005 Danish cartoons of Mohammed and the 2008 Dutch short film *Fitna*, which highlighted violent passages in the Koran. The Pakistani approach wasn't exactly subtle. According to Pakistan's *Daily Times*, the "delegation would also tell the EU that if such acts against Islam are not controlled, more attacks on the EU diplomatic missions abroad could not be ruled out."

Everybody got that? We're asking you nicely not to make any movies or cartoons that depict us as violent. And if you don't listen to us, there just might be more violence. Or, more concisely: Nice continent you've got there. Shame if anything were to happen to it.

Jordan, considered to be one of the more moderate Muslim countries, is getting in on the action too. Its Prosecutor General has brought charges against Geert Wilders, the Dutch member of parliament who produced *Fitna.* If Wilders refuses to go to Jordan to stand trial, international warrants will be issued for his arrest.

The plaintiff in the Jordanian lawsuit is Zakaria Al-Sheikh, head of something called the "Messenger of Allah Unites US Campaign." According to the Washington-based Center for Security Policy, Al-Sheikh called his suit "the first step towards setting in place an international law criminalizing anyone who insults Islam and the Prophet Mohammed." In the meantime, Al-Sheikh is rallying Jordanians to boycott products made in Holland and Denmark unless the manufacturers denounce the "Islamophobes."

The use of lawfare against the West isn't a new idea. The Koran itself describes various tactics used by Mohammed that could be seen as a form of "soft jihad" – tactical moves that promoted his conquests when military means were temporarily impractical. Islamic concepts such as *taqiyya* (strategic deception) and *hudna* (a short-term truce to be observed until the balance of power favours the Muslims) are part of this approach.

The "hard jihad" has not had a good run lately: The U.S. surge in Iraq, coming alongside the anti-terror "awakening" movement among the region's Sunni tribes, has meant setbacks for al Qaeda and its local allies. The most obvious difference between soft and hard jihad is that soft jihad doesn't involve physical violence. But there's another difference: Soft jihad works only with the willing co-operation of the West's human rights agencies, courts and NGOs. And so, for now, the soft jihad is where the action is – from Saudi money pouring into Western universities; to the Council of American-Islamic Relations lobbying Hollywood to change the bad guys in the film version of Tom Clancy's *The Sum of All Fears* from Muslim terrorists to neo-Nazis; to the UN's virulently anti-Semitic Durban conferences. Islamist lawfare is a growing international trend, and Canada's human rights commissions have unwittingly assumed a starring role.

This kind of co-opting has also been used by proponents of other ideologies. Vladimir Lenin, the first Communist dictator, talked about the "useful idiots of the West" who supported the Soviet Union for whatever addled reason. Lenin marvelled that so many people living in democratic nations would assist a dictatorial project aimed at world domination.

One of the most memorable letters the *Western Standard* received after reprinting the Danish cartoons of Mohammed came from a radical lesbian lawyer and activist in Vancouver named barbara findlay (she does not use capital letters in her name). findlay was a subscriber to my magazine, but when she heard that we were printing the cartoons, she immediately wrote to cancel her subscription – before the offending magazine even arrived in her mailbox. (findlay was one of the very few subscribers who cancelled; more than a thousand new subscribers signed up as an act of solidarity with us, including a startling number of Muslim and Arab Canadians.)

I immediately wrote back to findlay, refusing to accept her cancellation. Didn't she know, I pointed out, that she was allying herself with radical fascists, who would regard her sexual orientation – and her feminism in general – as an abomination? Didn't she know that the punishment for homosexuality in countries such as Saudi Arabia and Iran is execution? How could she side with those medieval fascists against freedom of speech?

findlay refused to debate me on the issue. But based on her track record of radical activism, I have a hunch I understand her thinking. Radical Islam today is what the Soviet Union was during the Cold War: the chief counterweight to the West. Back in the day, left-wing activists, philosophers, student demonstrators, and other malcontents who loathed their own democratic, capitalist society were moved to idealize the U.S.S.R. – the West's enemy – as a workers' paradise. They did this despite the fact that were they to practise their own brand of activism within the Soviet Union, it would have earned them a death sentence.

But what also weighed in support of some who shared the decision was the post-9/11 equivalent of this deluded Cold War intellectual strategy. A Western lesbian woman surely wouldn't want to live under sharia law – or support anyone who embraced that goal. But on an emotional level, her sympathies might instinctively lie with any ideological force that seeks to destabilize and counter what she sees as the white, Christian, capitalist patriarchy that rules our society – even a brown, Islamist, anti-gay, totalitarian patriarchy. The fact that lesbians would be the first ones for execution if the Islamists ever took power did not deter some lesbians from supporting the same position as radical Islam.

Not all "useful idiots" are radical. Many simply make the mistake of abandoning their own liberal values in the face of radical Islam, as a badge of multicultural tolerance. Too many feminists remain silent in the face of Islamic honour killings and polygamy – including right here in Canada – for fear of being called intolerant if they speak up. Too many gay rights activists, too many secular humanists are afraid to assert their own values of the separation of religion and state. I call this the "soft bigotry" of low expectations: holding Muslims to a lower standard than other ideological movements. It's political correctness, to be sure. But it corrodes the very foundations of our liberal society.

Great achievements in human rights – such as the equality of men and women; such as the acknowledgement that we should solve national problems without violence; such as our belief in pluralism, whereby each of us can choose our own religion (or none at all) – are not wins that last forever. If the attack on those values were to come through a military jihad, we'd know to fight back and rally to our national principles of freedom. But when those who challenge our way of life come not with a suicide bomber's vest but with letterhead marked "Human Rights Commission," we let down our guard.

Chapter 7

THE DANISH CARTOONS

Early on the morning of February 13, 2006, nearly forty thousand copies of the *Western Standard* magazine rolled off the presses in Edmonton. The cover story was about the power of political lobbyists in Ottawa. But tucked inside the magazine, on pages 15 and 16, was a story about a Danish newspaper that had commissioned a dozen cartoonists to draw the Muslim prophet Mohammed, and the chain of events that followed.

That Danish newspaper, the *Jyllands-Posten*, was making a point about the West's fear of insulting Islam. A Danish author and long-time leftist activist named Kåre Bluitgen had written a children's book about Mohammed. But because visual depictions of the Muslim prophet are taboo in Islam, Bluitgen found it difficult to find an illustrator. According to Bluitgen, the first three artists he approached refused, one referring to the murder of Dutch filmmaker Theo van Gogh by a Muslim radical, another citing the beating of a Danish lecturer by a Muslim gang for reading portions of the Koran to non-Muslims during a lecture. The *Jyllands-Posten* wanted to highlight the culture of self-censorship afflicting Denmark, and to show the newspaper's support for freedom of speech, by publishing twelve cartoons of Mohammed themselves.

The twelve cartoons were a mixed bag. One was exactly what Bluitgen had been looking for – a picture of Mohammed in a desert, walking with a donkey, the sort of image you'd see in an illustrated children's Bible. Another was a stylized version of Mohammed wearing a turban, combined with the Islamic crescent moon and star. It looked like a corporate logo. There were several in this vein – politically neutral, merely artistic impressions of an important historical figure. Other images mocked the *Jyllands-Posten* and Bluitgen himself, suggesting the whole thing was a PR stunt to sell more of his books. One of these cartoons featured a young Danish-born Muslim student writing on a chalkboard that the *Jyllands-Posten* was being provocative. The Mohammed in that picture wasn't the historical Mohammed, just a young Danish student.

A few of the cartoons were critical of radical Islam – but the criticism wasn't any harsher than that heaped on any other religion or ideology in the editorial cartoons of Western newspapers. One showed Mohammed in heaven, saying, "Stop, stop, we ran out of virgins!" as suicide bombers floated up to the clouds – a poke at the promise of seventy-two celestial virgins offered by radical Muslims in their terrorist-recruitment efforts. Another cartoon showed Mohammed wearing a turban that was in the shape of a bomb.

The cartoons were published by *Jyllands-Posten* in September 2005, but they didn't make international news until the next year. That was when a group of Danish imams went on a world tour to drum up Muslim anger against Denmark, bringing with them the twelve cartoons that were published plus three cartoons that they added themselves.

Those three extras – which hadn't been published in Denmark or anywhere else – were grotesque, including one showing Mohammed having sex with a dog. They were the imams' own handiwork, added to the bundle just in case the original cartoons didn't get the desired response.

In 2006, other developments in international affairs made these cartoons politically useful in parts of the Muslim world. Rafik Hariri, the former prime minister of Lebanon, was assassinated by a massive car bomb, and a UN investigation pointed the blame directly at Syria. At the same time, Iran's plan to develop nuclear weapons was beginning to marginalize that country diplomatically. The cartoons – which had been ignored until then – became a means for demagogic governments in Tehran, Damascus, and other radical Muslim nations to deflect attention from their own problems.

Suddenly, Syria and Iran witnessed riots – resulting in, among other outrages, the torching of Denmark's embassy in Damascus. That was quite an interesting development, given that neither Syria nor Iran tolerates freedom of assembly, let alone high-profile street violence. The most likely explanation is that both rallies had been orchestrated by the secret police.

Until that moment, the phrase *cartoon violence* had summoned to mind images of Wile E. Coyote fighting the Road Runner. But the spring of 2006 saw more than one hundred people die in purportedly spontaneous riots in response to the Danish cartoons. And a half-dozen terrorist plots to avenge the cartoons were uncovered across Europe.

The riots were huge news in and of themselves. But then a second news story developed – on the Internet and talk radio at least. Every newspaper and TV station in the Western world was covering the story of the riots, but almost none of them showed the cartoons themselves. Canada's own CBC TV was typical: the network refused to show the cartoons, they said, out of "respect" for Islam. It marked possibly the first time that network – home of such scathingly anti-Christian epics as *The Boys of St. Vincent* – censored the news because of religious sensitivity. Canada's other networks joined in the news boycott too. If curious Canadians wanted to see what the fuss was about, they'd have to do the work themselves, hunting for the cartoons on the Internet.

The media's self-censorship was based on the same fear exhibited by Denmark's illustrators. It played perfectly into the agenda of the radical Danish imams, who'd made the claim that the cartoons represented an off-limits insult to their religion. Canadians are used to all sorts of offensive broadcasts and publications coming their way, so it was fair for the public to assume that if editors and producers censored newsworthy cartoons out of respect, they must have been spectacularly vile – perhaps vile enough to stir reasonable people to riot. This was the message being sent to a misinformed public.

As a journalist, I found this cowardice masquerading as sensitivity to be appalling. I was publisher of the *Western Standard* at the time, a conservative news magazine with a reputation for political incorrectness – our motto was "tells it like it is." Our editor, Kevin Libin, and I knew that this was exactly the kind of story that our readers would be interested in – it touched on freedom of speech, the war on terror, political correctness, and violence. Our readers would want to see what all the fuss was about for themselves, and to be treated like grown-ups – not children kept out of an R-rated movie.

But Libin and I also felt that, being a fortnightly magazine, we would probably be beaten to the punch. The Sun Media tabloid chain would surely publish the cartoons eventually – they love controversial stories and pride themselves on being politically incorrect. The *National Post* had always been interested in issues related to radical Islam. And *Maclean's* magazine, since 2005 under the direction of conservative publisher-editor Ken Whyte, would probably take a crack at the subject too, we thought. It was one of those times when publishing every two weeks meant we'd miss the scoop.

Assuming that we'd be beaten to the publication of the cartoons themselves by one of our competitors, we took a more reflective approach. We asked experts: What did Islam really have to say about depicting Mohammed? Many branches of Islam, we noted, have a tradition of depicting Mohammed through the visual arts. In addition to reprinting eight of the twelve *Jyllands-Posten* cartoons, we ran a photo of an ancient Shiite mosaic of Mohammed.

As our publication date drew nearer, we couldn't help but notice that no other mainstream publication in Canada was going to press with the cartoons. We'd be the first, and possibly the only ones. We sent the magazine to our printers on Friday for printing over the weekend. The next day, word somehow leaked out. By Sunday, our decision to publish the cartoons was national news – even though nobody except our staff and our printers had even seen the spread.

I must have done a hundred interviews that week about our decision, and each one started out exactly the same way, with me being asked by other journalists why we did it. My response was the same every time, and it was heartfelt: "We published the cartoons because they were central to the biggest news story of the day, and we're a news magazine." I often followed that up with a question of my own: "You're a journalist. Why aren't you publishing them too?"

My very first interview would be particularly memorable, though it didn't seem that way at first. At 7 A.M. on Monday, while our magazine was being trucked from our printers to the post office, I appeared on CBC's *Eye Opener* radio show in Calgary. The amiable Jim Brown was the host, and the other guest was Syed Soharwardy. All I knew about him at the time was that he was a Pakistani immigrant to Canada who worked for IBM and had a part-time gig as a preacher at a tiny mosque in a strip mall in northeast Calgary. Soharwardy had very few followers – about forty congregants in a city of eighty thousand Muslims. But he was a big-time media hound, always trolling around for interviews, while the city's real imams rolled their eyes.

I tried to be engaging, as I usually do on such panels. I explained the newsworthiness of the cartoons, and said that the *Western Standard* published them not as a political statement but as news. My staff and I were simply doing our job as reporters.

But Soharwardy apparently wasn't quite in synch with our Canadian concepts of freedom of the press and the separation of religion and state. He called me a "terrorist" for publishing the cartoons – a bit rich, coming from someone who, I later learned, does the radical Muslim lecture circuit in Saudi Arabia. And then he announced to startled CBC listeners that he was a direct descendant of Mohammed, and so he felt personally offended. I wasn't quite sure what to do with that one, so I kept on my message, saying that Soharwardy was welcome to follow the Koran as his law, but we were in Canada, not Saudi Arabia. People like me could publish whatever they liked.

I'll admit the debate wasn't particularly polite – in fact, it degenerated into a shouting match. But with other interviews to get to, I soon put the verbal fracas out of my mind. But not Soharwardy. He was used to fawning media treatment, bestowed by politically correct reporters delighted to have a spot of diversity in their news. He wasn't used to someone disagreeing with him, or calling him a radical. Back in Pakistan, where he had been a student at a radical madrassah, if someone had spoken out that way to the imams, they'd have been whipped. Back in Saudi Arabia, where he had lectured at an officially anti-Semitic university, my blasphemy might even have resulted in my head being cut off.His first stop was to the offices of the Calgary Police Service, where he demanded that I be arrested. The police were very polite, gently explaining to him that he wasn't in Saudi Arabia or Pakistan any more, and that police in Canada don't enforce the Koran, and that they don't get involved in political disputes. I later learned that Soharwardy didn't take no for an answer – until the crown prosecutor wrote Soharwardy a letter explaining why what we did was perfectly legal.

This only made Soharwardy more determined. He shopped his grievance around town until he found someone willing to hear it. The day after our debate, Soharwardy filled out a complaint form with the Alberta Human Rights and Citizenship Commission. It was accepted by the commission the next day.

Stop for a moment to think about that. If you could go back in time forty years and tell Alan Borovoy or his fellow civil libertarians that in the twenty-first century, the police would be more respectful of civil liberties than the human rights commissions, they wouldn't believe you.

The HRC sent me a copy of Soharwardy's complaint, and I confess that when I first saw it, I thought it was some sort of bureaucratic glitch. The police hadn't even bothered to contact me about Soharwardy's ramblings. Perhaps, I thought, the HRC was simply going through the motions before throwing Soharwardy's hand-scrawled complaint in the garbage.

Soharwardy's complaint was something to see: a mishmash of personal braggadocio, Islamic supremacism, and plain old whining – all handwritten in surprisingly broken English for someone who had been living in Canada for twenty years. It was riddled with spelling errors, including in my name and the name of my magazine. But the Islamofascist nature of his thinking shone through anyway.

"Ezra Lavant insulted me on air on CBC radio," read his complaint. "He also said that the hateful cartoons are justified to be published in his magazine Western Standards." And Soharwardy wasn't just mad at me and my magazine; he complained that "CBC, CTV and other media" dared to speak with me. The complaint contained some personal details too: "I am openly the follower and related to Prophet Muhammad."

Soharwardy wrote that our publication of the cartoons "have sighted violence, hate and discrimination against my family and me." Such incitement – I'm guessing that's what he meant by "sighted" – would have been quite a feat, given that the magazines hadn't yet landed in any mailboxes, and wouldn't be on newsstands for another week. But Soharwardy did include as proof of his claims a raft of emails he had received from the public, including a message calling him "excitable" and "humourless," and telling him to "laugh" a little more. Another email said that there "are many fine Muslims out there," but that radical Islam deserved to be mocked.

This was the "violence" that Soharwardy faced – ordinary Canadians telling him off for his cranky radicalism. He'd been made to look like a fool on the radio and was looking to shoot the messenger.

Soharwardy followed up his original complaint with a detailed list of legal arguments – but not from any Canadian law books. He cited passages from the Koran as his grounds for a complaint. And the HRC, that supposed bastion of human rights in our secular society, bought it. Soharwardy quoted a dozen verses from the Koran, and insisted to the HRC that "the respect and obedience to Prophet Muhammad is the most basic requirement of Faith."

I'm sure that cuts a lot of ice back in the madrassahs of Pakistan, or in the town squares in Saudi Arabia, right before they chop off the hands of thieves. But in Canada, respect for Mohammed – or any other religious figure – is not a "basic requirement" at all. We don't have a state religion, and the Koran isn't our constitution.

Soharwardy then quoted a passage from the Koran that had to do with death-deserving infidels. "Those who disbelieve make a false contention . . . they are warned for a mockery." Fair enough – I'll be sure to keep out of the man's mosque. But since when is enforcing the Koran's threats against infidels part of the HRC's mandate?

At the end of his letter of complaint, Soharwardy went through the cartoons, one by one, and gave both his artistic and religious criticism of each, adding: "I am quite disturbed and mentally tortured by these cartoons." And he was crystal clear about his demands: "I am expecting a formal apology . . . from the Western Standard. Please help."

Alberta's HRC was more than happy to help. But Soharwardy hasn't got his apology yet, and he never will.

I consulted with Tom Ross, a Calgary lawyer with experience dealing with HRC complaints. Ross said there were two ways to approach a complaint such as this – we could do what other clients would probably do, and try to make the problem go away quickly, possibly with a cash payment, an apology, and participation in a "re-education session." Or we could fight like hell. After that initial conversation, we didn't waste any time talking about option one.

I was outraged that a government agency was actually getting involved with the editorial decisions of our magazine. Still, I remained under the delusion that all the attention being paid Soharwardy was merely a bureaucratic formality – the result of some rule or other that said Alberta's HRC had to bring any complaint to my attention, no matter how ridiculous.

The *Western Standard* was, of course, prepared to debate our decision to run the cartoons. But that would be a voluntary process, one involving our subscribers (they loved our decision to publish the images); our advertisers (they were nervous at first, but stood with us); and our distributors (most stood with us – and saw strong newsstand sales). In our very next edition after the cartoons, we ran an extended letters-to-the-editor section, with the entire spectrum of views represented, from nutbars who said I only published the cartoons because I was Jewish, to a worried mother of a Canadian soldier in Afghanistan, to a Muslim immigrant to Canada who said she wanted to get away from sharia law, not have it follow her across the sea.

That's what a public debate looks like – in Canada, at least. Soharwardy didn't participate. He wanted a sharia-style solution.

Six weeks after we published the cartoons, when members of the public had already chewed the issues over and made up their minds, when the commotion was dying down, and we decided to let our extra security staff go – there hadn't been a single incident, and they had become well-armed, well-paid doormen – I got around to writing the *Western Standard's* reply to Soharwardy's complaint.

Rereading my words three years later, I realize that, back then, I still didn't understand how much trouble I was in, and how lopsided the human rights system truly was. My reply was earnest and full of good-faith appeals to common sense. It got me nowhere. All in all, I ended up being investigated for nine hundred days by the HRC, which, according to Access to Information documents I've received, had no fewer than fifteen government bureaucrats working my case. I was a major crime scene. It now seems laughable that I once thought that if I just explained things to the HRC, common sense would prevail.

Here's how I started my written response:

> The complaint is a frivolous and vexatious abuse of process. It has no basis in fact or Canadian law. It is contrary to Canadian values of freedom of speech, freedom of the press and religious plurality, under which Canadians are free from compulsion to submit to religious edicts. The complaint is an attempt to abuse the power of the state to chill discussion about subjects that are in the public interest. It is also an inappropriate combination of mosque and state, using a secular government agency to enforce a Muslim religious precept, namely the fundamentalist prohibition of the depiction of Mohammed.

I still believe every word of that. It's just slightly embarrassing that, in my youthful naïveté, I actually thought those enunciated principles mattered. As I learned since, the right not to be offended trumps freedom of speech in Alberta – that's the official position of the Government of Alberta, as argued by their lawyer David Kamal in the aforementioned *Lund v. Boissoin* case. And AHRCC Commissioner Lori Andreachuk made Kamal's arguments into law.

"If the [Alberta Human Rights and Citizenship Commission] does not dismiss this complaint, as did the Calgary Police Service in response to a similar complaint brought by the same complainant, the AHRCC will be discredited and its liberal reputation will be brought into disrepute. This complaint perverts the cause of human rights," I continued.

> If the AHRCC allows itself to be used to attack the publication of a good faith debate on these issues, the AHRCC will become a tool of censorship akin to libel chill. If it does not dismiss this complaint, the AHRCC will send a message that the state, with its unlimited resources, will not hesitate to interfere with and harass media that discuss controversial topics even in a bona fide manner.

Unfortunately, I got that part right. A year later, in March 2007, *Maclean's* magazine was hauled before three HRCs to answer for its discussion of radical Islam. And a year after that, a Christian pastor was given a lifelong ban against preaching any sermon that took a politically incorrect view of homosexuality. There is no more public debate allowed on those issues – the HRCs have said so.

I even had an eerie premonition about how much this complaint was going to cost me. "Even an acquittal, therefore, is a punishment. The process becomes the penalty." I had no idea, however, that the complaint would stretch on for three years and cost me six figures. That fact helps explain why so many people roll over when faced with a human rights complaint – my lawyer's "option one."

Soon after I sent in my response, I was hit with an almost identical complaint by the Edmonton Council of Muslim Communities. They filed a letter that was almost identical to Soharwardy's, but with fewer typos, and they submitted emails that Soharwardy had personally received. They weren't even pretending that it was anything more than strategic piling on.

Eight months passed, and I heard nothing. The AHRCC were clearly flummoxed. I wasn't following their game plan of surrendering and begging for mercy. I'd done the opposite: I dug in my heels, and even published the complaints (and my responses) – on the *Western Standard*'s website.

The HRC offered to set up a "conciliation meeting" in which I would sit down with Soharwardy and the Edmonton radicals and try to hash things out. I told the commission that there could be only one form of "conciliation" that I would accept: that these complainants reconcile themselves to Canadian values, and leave their fascist, Saudi-style approach to free speech overseas.

For some reason, that response wasn't well received – so the *Dr. Phil*–style meeting was cancelled.

The AHRCC's next move was to offer me a plea bargain: The human rights commission told Ross that if I agreed to publish an apology in the magazine and pay a few thousand dollars to the complainants, I could walk free. I replied that I would fight the AHRCC and their hijackers all the way to the Supreme Court before I did that – and even if I lost there, I'd contemplate doing jail time for contempt of court before apologizing.

Another four months passed. Seasons came and went. I started to wonder whether my growling had scared off the AHRCC. No – they were simply moving at the speed of government. One year after I had rejected their terms of surrender, they told Ross that they were moving to the next phase, the formal "investigation." I was to present myself to a "human rights officer" to be interrogated about my decision as publisher to print the controversial cartoons.

It was really happening: I had become the first journalist in the free world to be grilled by a government inquisitor about the cartoons. Not even the Danish cartoonists themselves were called in to answer for what they'd done. Nor had any of the newspapers throughout Europe that had republished the cartoons in solidarity with the *Jyllands-Posten*. I had the dubious honour of being a pioneer in the burgeoning field of Western Islamo-censorship.

It was a delicate matter. If I refused the AHRCC's "invitation" to be interrogated, its officers, under Section 23 of the Alberta Human Rights Citizenship and Multiculturalism Act, could enter my office without a search warrant and seize any "records and documents, including electronic records and documents, that are or may be relevant to the subject matter of the investigation" and "remove any of the things . . . for the purpose of making copies of or extracts from them."

Computer hard drives, confidential files, private correspondence, even letters between me and my lawyer could be seized. There are no exceptions, not even for information traditionally regarded as privileged by real courts. And all this could be done without a search warrant. And Section 24 of the act allows AHRCC employees to ask a judge – on their own initiative, without having to give notice to the person being investigated – for permission to enter my home to take whatever they like there too.

Ross spent weeks negotiating the terms of my interrogation. I wanted to go to the interrogation with magazine staff, including our former editor Kevin Libin, not just with my lawyer. I also wanted the interrogation to be a public proceeding, open to the media. The human rights officer in charge of my investigation, Shirlene McGovern, refused to allow me to bring anyone but Ross and my nine months' pregnant wife. Media were barred from the room too. But McGovern did agree to allow us to record the proceedings.

After weeks of haggling over the details, the interrogation was on – scheduled for Friday, January 11, 2008, nearly two full years after we first published the cartoons. In fact, the *Western Standard* magazine itself had ceased publishing three months earlier for unrelated business reasons, though the charges were still being prosecuting against the surviving company, and against me as its president.

The meeting was held at my lawyer's office in downtown Calgary. A gaggle of reporters showed up and camped out despite being told that they couldn't enter. I showed up early to check out the room and to go over last-minute details with Ross. We set up a video camera and tested it. I took my seat and my wife sat down by the camera.

When McGovern arrived, a middle-aged woman dressed in casual clothes, I did not think she looked particularly intimidating. In fact, she was smiling and chatty, and immediately reached out her hand to shake mine.

I was taken aback by her gesture: I had been trapped in HRC red tape for two years because of a nuisance suit, I had incurred enormous costs, and now I was about to be grilled by some government bureaucrat about my political and religious views. And if I didn't participate, my office and house could be raided and my computers and papers might be seized. All for publishing some cartoons. Would you have shaken hands with her?

I didn't, and I told her why: This wasn't a social visit. It wasn't voluntary on my part. If we'd met on the street as two strangers, I'd have been friendly to her. But this was part of an adversarial process whose aim was to extinguish my most fundamental constitutional rights.

Then McGovern spotted the video camera, and she hesitated for a moment. She'd agreed that I could record the proceedings but hadn't explicitly consented to videotaping. McGovern had a choice to make: cancel the interrogation over this point of procedure or just get the thing over with. It was Friday afternoon, and perhaps the path of least resistance beckoned. With a shrug, she agreed to the videotape. It was a decision she would come to regret.

McGovern had a few notes jotted down – questions she was planning to ask me, most of which had already been answered exhaustively in my formal legal response nearly two years earlier. I was prepared too – with an opening statement that I read to her in an admittedly angry tone.

"When the *Western Standard* magazine printed the Danish cartoons of Mohammed two years ago, I was the publisher. It was the proudest moment of my public life," I said. "I would do it again today," I continued. "In fact, I did do it again today. Though the *Western Standard*, sadly, no longer publishes a print edition, I posted the cartoons this morning on my website, EzraLevant.com."

It was a proud moment for me. I'd be willing to bet that not a single victim of a hate speech complaint, at either the federal or provincial level, has had the chutzpah to republish the material that got them in trouble on the very morning of their interrogation – and to tell their interrogator about it. It was more refined than telling McGovern to f-off, but it had the same effect. She was stunned.

"I am here at this government interrogation under protest," I continued.

> It is my position that the government has no legal or moral authority to interrogate me or anyone else for publishing these words and pictures. That is a violation of my ancient and inalienable freedoms: freedom of speech, freedom of the press, and in this case, religious freedom and the separation of mosque and state. It is especially perverted that a bureaucracy calling itself the Alberta human rights commission would be the government agency violating my human rights. So I will now call those bureaucrats "the commission" or "the HRC," since to call the commission a "human rights commission" is to destroy the meaning of those words.

McGovern, who'd by now apparently accustomed herself to my show of pride and fury, rolled her eyes. This was supposed to be her interrogation, a chance for her to hold the stick and for me to be the piñata. But I kept going. I told McGovern that "the commission is a joke – it's the Alberta equivalent of a U.S. television pseudo-court such as *Judge Judy* – except that Judge

Judy actually was a judge, whereas none of the commission's panellists are judges, and some aren't even lawyers. And, unlike the commission, Judge Judy believes in freedom of speech."

I quoted the great Alan Borovoy. He recently had come out and specifically condemned the complaints against me as abusive. I called the AHRCC a violation of 800 years of British common law, and two hundred and fifty years of Canadian law too, including our 1960 Bill of Rights and our Charter of Rights. I even quoted from the 1948 United Nations Universal Declaration of Human Rights, which protects free speech.

"I have no faith in this farcical commission," I concluded. "But I do have faith in the justice and good sense of my fellow Albertans and Canadians. I believe that the better they understand this case, the more shocked they will be. I am here under your compulsion to answer the commission's questions. But it is not I who am on trial: It is the freedom of all Canadians. You may start your interrogation."

For the next ninety minutes, I think that for every minute McGovern spoke, I spoke for ten. I had made that decision in advance with Ross: if we were going to be hauled into a show trial, I said, let's make it our show. I made a passionate case against government censorship and against the Islamic fascists who had hijacked the HRCs.

Even at the time, I suspected it was all pointless from a strictly legal point of view, since no one had ever beaten a hate speech accusation at the Alberta Human Rights Commission (or at the Canadian Human Rights Commission, for that matter). Moreover, McGovern was the same investigator who'd gone after Rev. Stephen Boissoin. If the AHRCC was prepared to convict a man of the cloth, what chance did I stand? No, my defiance was aimed not at any bureaucrat but at the court of public opinion.

There were a few interesting things that McGovern said in between my outbursts. At the beginning of her interrogation, she said: "I always ask people . . . what was your intent and purpose of your article?" That sounds pretty harmless, but parse the words and you find it contains two explosive elements.

The first was her casual statement that she "always" asks people these questions. Always? Just how often does McGovern haul people in off the street for questioning about their politics? That's one of the mysteries about these star chambers; we know only about the cases in which the targets are stubborn enough to fight. The vast majority of them settle without a hearing. Asking questions was what McGovern – and who knows how many others at the AHRCC – did for a living.

The second was that she asked my "purpose and intent" behind publishing the cartoons. Now why would that be relevant? This was an interrogation; it wasn't a friendly chat. It appeared that how I answered a question about my private state of mind would have an impact on whether I'd be prosecuted. Our magazine article spoke for itself – the words and the pictures were what they were. What difference did it make what my own personal views were? Would the article be legal if I had happy thoughts but illegal if my thoughts somehow offended the commission and its politically correct sensibilities? It was bad enough – illegal enough, I'd say – for the government to haul me in to explain my deeds. But since when did the government have the right to summon me to ask me about my inner thoughts?

"You're entitled to your opinions, that's for sure," she declared cavalierly as the proceeding was rolling to a close. But that just wasn't true, was it? If I had been entitled to my opinions, I wouldn't have been summoned to a ninety-minute interrogation by the government on pain of having my office and home searched if I refused. And I wouldn't be standing accused in a human rights proceeding that could end with me being forced to pay tens of thousands of dollars and enduring who knows what humiliating punishments besides.

The whole meeting was like two totally different conversations that rarely intersected. She wasn't interested in debating civil rights or natural justice. She really couldn't care less about my appeals to our Canadian legal traditions. She was just systematically going through her checklist of bureaucratic questions, apparently unmoved my pleas and demands.

To her, this was just a day's work, be it with an unusually uncooperative target. She really didn't seem to have any doubt that what she was doing was perfectly normal and legitimate – and maybe even valuable to society. She genuinely thought that the government had the right to dragoon journalists into offices to answer questions about their private thoughts and "intentions."

When I got home, I watched the whole videotape of the interrogation. Then I spent the weekend uploading clips of my interrogation onto the Internet, using the video site YouTube. I emailed a couple of dozen friends about them – fellow journalists, family, and former colleagues from the *Western Standard.* I thought that the clips would get a thousand views, maybe ten thousand at most.

But as the days passed, the hit count grew. My fight became a symbol for free speech activists – and opponents of radical Islam – everywhere. That weekend, my "channel" on YouTube was the fifth-most-watched video site on the entire Internet. Within ten days, four hundred thousand people had watched the videos.

I started blogging about my experience and Stephen Taylor, my volunteer webmaster, suggested that I put a PayPal button up so that sympathetic Web surfers could contribute financially to my cause with the click of a button, since the magazine was no longer around to foot the bills. When I got the bill from my lawyers, I was able to cover it with the Internet donations, not my and my wife's savings (as she had feared).

The details of my case were interesting to some – especially since they showed how Islamic lawfare was set to hijack our legal system. But I think that whether the subject matter of the complaint had been Mohammed cartoons or Jesus cartoons, the outrage would have been the same. It simply wasn't normal for a government to grill a journalist about the state of his mind and the content of his magazine. It was shocking.

The resulting media storm felt reminded me of the reaction in February 2006, when we had first published the cartoons. But this time it was bigger, and the support I received was now more uniform. In 2006, many journalists had asked whether it was the right decision to publish the cartoons. A COMPAS survey of Canadian journalists found that 70 per cent of them agreed with our decision, but reasonable people could disagree. It was about an editorial judgment call.

Not this time. This time, it wasn't about whether we should have published the cartoons. It was about whether we had the right to do so. Even journalists and political pundits who took issue with our decision in 2006 stood firmly with us in 2008. They knew that if the government thought it could be not just the magazine's editor but mine too, as evidenced by their questions about my personal views and intentions – then nobody was safe.

The issue electrified the media. The Internet, of course, was on it first. That was partly because I had uploaded the videos over the weekend, and the inhabitants of the blogosphere had a head start over the Monday-to-Friday journalists. Moreover, free speech is a core value for bloggers, many of whom consider themselves heterodox in their opinions. Blogs are a natural haven for political dissent.

Had I been charged with hate speech ten, even five, years ago, I don't know if I could have fought back as effectively. YouTube, which brought my story alive for six hundred thousand people by the time the traffic died down, debuted only in 2005. Before that, there was no universally surfed repository of current event–themed videos and bloggers were much less prevalent.

If all this had happened in 1996 instead of 2006, few would know anything about my battle. Even if I had videotaped the interrogation, so what? At most, I'd have been able to get a short excerpt aired on a TV newscast. Even if the people who saw it found it outrageous, there would have been no outlet through which to channel their anger.

And without the credit card donations made possible by PayPal, which was formed in 2000, it's unlikely that I could have mustered the war chest necessary to fight not only the two cartoon complaints against me, but also the subsequent defamation suits and law society complaints by both radical jihadists and the human rights industry, all of which came as a response to my criticisms.

In short, the Internet saved me. In that sense, my story isn't just about free speech. It's also about new technology – and the way it's levelled the playing field between big government and private citizens.

And as I will discuss in more detail in the next chapter, the Internet may also spell the beginning of the end for the HRCs.

In the days after my hearing, I began to blog about human rights commissions and free speech, encouraged by the world-wide support I had received, both moral and financial. EzraLevant.com became one of the five most popular political blogs in Canada. The support I got through Internet, which soon crossed over into the mainstream media, reassured me that I was the "normal" one – that free speech was normal, that resisting government nosiness was normal – and that it was the human rights commission that stood as an affront to our Western values.

Within ten days of my YouTube videos going global, the human rights commission wrote to my lawyer saying that McGovern had quit my case citing the enormous backlash against her. Although McGovern's performance was just another day at the office for her, to hundreds of thousands of people around the world, the HRC had become a hated symbol of government censorship. It all must have seemed so shocking to a low-level bureaucrat.

Soharwardy, too, came under enormous scrutiny. He'd always styled himself as the friendly neighbourhood imam. But all of a sudden, with thousands of bloggers figuratively jumping down his throat, he wasn't in control of his own media image. Even the local Calgary newspapers, which used to dutifully go to Soharwardy for explanations of the significance of Muslim holidays, were asking him tough questions. It wasn't long before Soharwardy's past comments were dug up – his call for all Canadians to live under sharia law and his outrageous accusation that Western aid agencies were kidnapping Muslim children.

Soharwardy's tiny mosque made headlines too. Half of the roughly forty congregants were up in arms against him, demanding to know what he had done with their donations and why he hadn't filed financial statements as required by law. As I mentioned earlier, Soharwardy also was accused of harassment by two female congregants. Suddenly, he'd become a scary figure – a Pakistani-Saudi radical whose critics became the subject of poisonous vendettas.

So Soharwardy started a PR campaign to rehabilitate his image. In early 2008, he asked for an editorial board meeting with the *Calgary Herald*, the largest newspaper in the city. And there he pled his case as a "moderate" who was simply misunderstood. But his campaign backfired spectacularly. The editorial board came armed with evidence of Soharwardy's own track record of intolerance. Instead of swooning before him as they normally did, they grilled him for nearly two hours.

As Licia Corbella, the *Herald*'s editorial board editor, wrote afterwards, "Soharwardy is a charmer. He convinced me that I must have misread his columns. But relistening to the tape of our meeting and rereading his original texts, one thing is clear: He cannot be believed." Corbella calmly listed his lies and deceptions and ever-changing excuses. "Changing his words, as is his way, won't likely be the salve to his reputation that he's looking for this time," she concluded.

Within three weeks, Soharwardy had abandoned his complaint against me – sticking taxpayers with the approximately $500,000 tab for the AHRCC's investigation and me and the *Western Standard* with the better part of $100,000 in expenses. He just walked away, without a penny of penalties or even an apology. A few months later, with Soharwardy out of the picture, the AHRCC quietly snuffed out the piggyback complaint from the Edmonton Council of Muslim Communities. I'd won – even if it didn't feel like a victory.

As Soharwardy told CBC's *The National*, "People were looking at Ezra Levant as a martyr of freedom of his speech . . . taking this into a different direction that I did not want." No kidding. Soharwardy wanted to use Alberta's Human Rights and Citizenship Commission as a weapon to bully me, a critic of radical Islam who had embarrassed him on CBC radio two years earlier. And he did bully me, in the kangaroo court. But in the court of public opinion, he had self-detonated.

Within a few months, he left town, telling journalists that he was going on a cross-country "multi-faith" walk against violence. He was leaving behind a city that had its fill of his hypocrisy, a little mosque that was crumbling under lawsuits and investigations, and unanswered questions about the physical violence that had befallen two of his fiercest critics. Good riddance.

None of that would have happened had I not videotaped my interrogation and set loose the result onto YouTube. I was the one who was supposed to crumple under the weight of a politically correct accuser and the fifteen bureaucrats at the AHRCC he managed to co-opt. Instead, McGovern quit and Soharwardy abandoned his complaint – and the city.

For the first time in more than two years, I felt as if my allies and I might win this fight – not just the narrow legal struggle about publishing a bunch of cartoons, but the larger fight for our freedom.

Chapter 8

AN ARMY OF DAVIDS

The year 2008 started off like any other year for Canada's HRCs – big budgets, big powers, and not a lot of accountability. Parliament and the provincial legislatures pretty much let the HRCs do what they wanted. And the media, with a few notable exceptions, were oblivious to their very existence. Occasionally, a particularly motivated or well-financed victim of the HRCs would appeal an unfair decision to a higher court and get a nutty ruling struck down. But life at the human rights commissions could fairly have been called placid.

There isn't any polling data on the subject, but I'd estimate from my own travels that before my interrogation at the Alberta Human Rights and Citizen Commission, Mark Steyn's show trial at the BCHRT, and the other cases that made the news in 2008, 99 per cent of Canadians wouldn't even have known what a human rights commission was. That's certainly not the case today. Canadians are now asking questions about Canada's

HRCs – even questioning whether we still need these 1960s-era relics at all.

In terms of the legal precedents they set in 2008, the HRCs have never been more dangerous: the Stalinist lifetime ban on Rev. Stephen Boissoin's preaching; the asinine ruling to commit comedian Guy Earle to trial; the direct assault on the freedom of the mainstream media in the trial of Mark Steyn and *Maclean's*.

And things are likely to get worse. Just ask Barbara Hall, the chief commissioner of the Ontario Human Rights Commission, Canada's second-biggest HRC. On Canada Day 2008, the Ontario rules changed. Now all complaints go straight to a hearing at the tribunal – nothing is screened out in advance, and there are no longer any limits to the amount that can be awarded for "pain and suffering." It's like a new Ontario lottery, except that you don't even need to pay for a ticket. Hall says she wants the number of complaints in Ontario to "spike" under the new rules. As she wrote in a public letter, she's on the hunt for "known and unknown causes of discrimination." I guess she'll have to invent discrimination no one has ever heard of before, if that's what it takes to keep her little government fiefdom staffed and funded.

Fewer obstacles to making a complaint, bigger paydays for winning. It's certainly a recipe for more human rights litigation. But things were already going in that direction. Each exorbitant new HRC ruling adds to the case law, setting another precedent. And it also acts as an advertisement for more complaints. In 2004, the AHRCC awarded Ruby Repas $4,900 when she was fired as the kitchen manager from Albert's Family Restaurant after contracting hepatitis. Three and a half years later, Beena Datt was awarded more than $50,000 from the BCHRT when McDonald's let her go for medical reasons because she couldn't wash her hands as often as McDonald's required. That's a ten-fold increase for the same sort of "discrimination" by restaurants who try to remove health risks.

But in politics, no less than in physics, every action provokes an equal and opposite reaction. As the HRCs get bolder in their choice of targets, media attention increases and public skepticism becomes more pronounced. And even some of the less obvious flaws in the HRCs – such as their lack of proper procedure or the fact that complaints can be shopped around from HRC to HRC – have started to get attention now that those aspects have become so brazenly abused.

It took a while for the groundswell to get started, however. Though my interrogation had been a sensation on the Internet, not a single newspaper reported on the matter, except for the *National Post*, in a brief item. There was some frustration brewing in the blogosphere, where news cycles move very quickly – much faster even than at any TV station. Bloggers had chewed over my case, done their research, and come to the conclusion that the laws governing Canada's HRCs needed to be changed. But the mainstream media seemed oblivious to the issue – and so did the elected legislators who have the power to change the laws.

I worked on Parliament Hill in the late 1990s as the legislative assistant to a political party leader, so I know a little about how things work in Ottawa. Parliament almost never moves quickly. Away from the sound and fury of question period, the ruling party's usual response to any problem is to study it. And more often than not, that is where things end. Given all the citizens groups and interest groups who are active on the Hill, even getting a politician's attention is difficult. MPs don't open their own mail – their staff do it for them and give occasional reports about what's hot back home. Standard form replies are sent. I faced the same problem that any advertiser faces when trying to sell a product: How do you get through all of the other noise?

On January 16, 2008, five days after I had been interrogated, I laid out a very simple plan for the small army of Internet activists who had begun to gather at my website every day looking to do something about HRCs other than just complain in the blogosphere. It was a simple suggestion about how to move from talking among ourselves to making real changes. Eight words, actually:

1. Denormalize the commissions; and
2. Press legislators to act.

Given the positive associations people have with the broad concept of human rights, it has to be done in that order. Notwithstanding their misleading name, human rights commissions have to be revealed as the un-Canadian organizations they are. Only when their reputation is damaged will enterprising politicians dare to tackle them. Usually, political leaders wait until they can tell which way the winds are blowing before coming out with a strong opinion. Not because they are unprincipled, but because they only have so much political capital, and so they have to choose their battles.

Battling against a government entity whose name contains the words *human rights* was particularly going to be tough for Stephen Harper's Conservative government, which oversees the largest of the fourteen HRCs. In 2008, they had a minority government that was constantly at risk of toppling. Given the opposition's endless efforts to portray Harper as an anti–human rights reactionary, why would the prime minister invite another controversy? If any politician was going to act, a lot of spadework had to be done first.

Single-issue political campaigns are difficult to promote without the infrastructure and money of a political party behind them. How do you inform thirty-three million Canadians about HRCs? How to you expose the bad behaviour of the commissions – especially their often-subtle perversions of the law? Idea campaigns such as that can cost millions of dollars. And even then – as the "Yes" campaign for the 1992 Charlottetown Accord referendum proved – that isn't always enough.

As it turned out, the Internet – which had picked up on my battle from the earliest days – would prove the perfect tool. There wouldn't be any door-knocking or any mass rallies. Instead, the action would be online – at EzraLevant.com, FiveFeetofFury.com, SmallDeadAnimals.com, BlazingCatFur.blogspot.com, and other Canadian blogs – where a growing group of anti-HRC activists met to exchange news tips, documents, and expertise. Over time, various journalists from the mainstream media became part of the community too – using the blogosphere as a source for scoops and story ideas. It turns out I no longer had to worry about my story jumping from the Web to the media. Increasingly, the two are one and the same – even if it sometimes takes print and broadcast journalists a few weeks to cotton on to stories that bloggers jump on in a matter of hours, even minutes.

Mark Steyn, the internationally published political commentator, started writing about HRCs on a regular basis on his own popular website, especially after *Maclean's* magazine was sued by the Canadian Islamic Congress because they published an excerpt from his book. His campaign also spawned FreeMarkSteyn.com, a one-stop website with links to every story about human rights commissions published in the country.

Ten years ago, such a press clippings service would have been available only to well-funded political operations that hire professional media monitoring companies. But in this age, anyone with an Internet connection can set up a "Google alert" to automatically be sent an email when key words such as *human rights commission* or even *Ezra Levant* show up on any of the thousands of news sources monitored by Google.

In short, the anti-HRC groundswell was what pioneering blogger Glenn Reynolds of Instapundit.com called "An Army of Davids." In his 2006 book by that title, Reynolds argued that technology has broken the monopoly that the Goliaths of business and politics once had over decision making. One little blogger on his or her own may not be able to do much – but allied with dozens or even hundreds of others, that blogger can move even the mightiest companies or governments. And that's exactly what happened with HRCs, even though most of the "Davids" fighting against the HRC Goliaths have never met each other, and likely never will. Five months after my videotaped interrogation, Jennifer Lynch, the chief commissioner of the Canadian Human Rights Commission, told the *National Post* that the "velocity" of the public response "took all of us by surprise."

Some bloggers approached the issue from a religious freedom point of view, others from a libertarian point of view, others as a purely political issue. One musically inclined activist, Jed Marlin, wrote hilarious songs about human rights commissions. A man named Wally Keeler came up with biting graphics and posters. Some bloggers who also happened to be lawyers analyzed rulings from HRCs.

The first political breakthrough came on January 30, 2008, when Keith Martin, an MP from Vancouver Island, introduced a private member's motion to Parliament's Order Paper. It was just one sentence long: "That, in the opinion of the House, subsection 13(1) of the Canadian Human Rights Act should be deleted from the Act." That provision of the CHRA is what gives the federal HRC jurisdiction to prosecute hate speech complaints. Most private member's motions never make it to a vote. Martin's didn't either. His motion, M-446, was a symbolic gesture reflecting his own personal opinion. Still, it was a landmark event.

But Martin wasn't just any MP. He was a Liberal MP – a tremendously important fact, given that the highest-profile victims of the HRCs had been political conservatives such as Mark Steyn and me. Martin is also a medical doctor and a visible minority. (He jokingly referred to himself as "coffee-coloured.") And as a member of the Médecins sans Frontières charity, he had solid human rights credentials.

Martin's participation in the campaign against the HRCS helped neutralize the attack that the human rights industry often mounts against its critics: With a self-described coffee-coloured Liberal MP standing up for me, a Jew with conservative political beliefs, it was pretty tough for the forces of the status quo to present the anti-HRC camp as closet bigots in league with neo-Nazis.

Immediately, the "Army of Davids" sent letters and emails to MPs across the country, pressing them on whether they'd support Martin's motion. My website became a clearinghouse for such news, and whenever an MP said something encouraging – even just a little – I'd publish the message on my blog, along with a flattering photo of the MP. Voters from across the country started faxing and emailing me copies of correspondence from their own MPs on the matter.

I'd always close the loop by encouraging my growing readership to send a quick email of encouragement to MPs who had taken a stand. Parliamentary staff told me that my modest call to arms resulted in as many as a hundred letters of congratulations being received by individual MPs in a single day – the sort of positive anomaly that would be sure to be immediately reported to the MP directly.

Unfortunately, the first widely read news report about Martin's motion was a shocking smear, written by Joan Bryden of the Canadian Press. It started with this sentence: "A Liberal MP is being hailed as a poster boy for free speech on a white supremacist website" – and it went downhill from there.

There was some truth to this statement. One of the thousands of websites that had weighed in for reform of the HRCs was Stormfront.org, which is, indeed, a white supremacist site (whose members, as I discussed earlier, included several staff at the CHRC). But Bryden's lengthy article didn't mention any of the other sources of support for Martin's motion across the spectrum of legitimate opinion. It was clear the reporter had an agenda; she couldn't paint Martin as a racist, but she could paint him as a dupe.

But Bryden overplayed her hand. In her article, she wrote that "Liberal Leader Stéphane Dion's office disavowed the motion and suggested Martin will be asked to withdraw it" – a claim that turned out to have been based on an interview with a low-level Liberal spin doctor, who acknowledged only that the motion didn't reflect the Liberal Party's view (which is, by definition, true of any private member's motion).

Enter Deborah Gyapong, part of the volunteer blogging army, Ottawa brigade. Gyapong's day job was reporter for a small Christian publication, a post that came with a Parliamentary Press Pass. Gyapong fact-checked Bryden's story by going to Parliament Hill and re-interviewing Martin. It turned out that Dion had not told him to withdraw the motion, as Bryden had suggested. In fact, Martin confirmed, his proposal was met with "huge" support by other Liberal MPs, and he planned to continue pressing the point.

Gyapong provided the kind of public fact-checking that would have been impossible just a few years ago. Even if she had been able to accost Martin on her own, what could she have done with that information before the age of blogs? As it happened, she posted her facts, and dozens of other blogs immediately linked to her site, outing CP's sloppy, biased reporting for what it was.

Other members of the blog army were more blunt: They emailed Bryden directly, challenging her neutrality. Bryden was taken aback – like the CHRC, she was surprised by the "velocity" of public discontent. One member of the public, Ken Moodie, demanded to know why the very first story – the very first words! – written by Bryden about the HRCs was an attempt making the opponents appear guilty by association with white supremacists, instead of dealing with the broader issue of HRC censorship itself. Bryden wrote Moodie an email – quickly circulated throughout the Internet – admitting that her spin had "generated considerable comment from readers who felt it was unfair and biased." Bryden admitted that her story was prompted by political spin doctors, and claimed in her defence that it was "not intended to be the definitive story investigating every angle of the controversy over the human rights act. It was a news story about a specific development that day." As Moodie pointed out, that excuse didn't hold water, as it was the first – and only – story Bryden wrote on the subject.

Just a few days later, another media breakthrough happened: The editorial board of the *Globe and Mail* wrote an unsigned editorial – the official view of the newspaper – condemning the human rights complaints against *Maclean's* magazine and me, and specifically praising Martin's motion. It closed with the sentence "It's time to rein [the HRCs] in before further damage is done to Canadians' right to free expression."

Plenty of columnists and talk radio hosts already had denounced the HRCs. But the *Globe and Mail* had, until then, been pretty silent. For that icon of respectability to come out so strongly against the HRCs meant that even cautious, dignified, old-school Toronto was fed up with the country's human rights mandarins. What had been a radical cause just weeks earlier had now gone mainstream.

That same week, PEN Canada, the high-minded literary organization dedicated to freedom of speech, issued a press release on the subject too. PEN mentioned both Mark Steyn and me by name and said, "Neither complaints should ever have been accepted by a human rights commission and both should be immediately dismissed." PEN didn't stop there: it demanded that the Section 13 hate speech section be struck from the CHRA, along with its counterpart provisions in provincial and territorial law.

The PEN statement was issued by Christopher Waddell, who also happened to be a working journalist at the CBC. The group's list of directors and advisors is a who's who of Canada's literati, from authors Margaret Atwood and the late June Callwood to filmmaker David Cronenberg to actress Susan

Coyne. Their honorary patron is John Ralston Saul, the husband of the former Governor General of Canada, Adrienne Clarkson. The little army of volunteer bloggers all of a sudden had some very fancy company.

Day in and day out, the "Army of Davids" exposed ridiculous HRC rulings as they were issued by the fourteen HRCs across the country. Those with a knack for research started working backwards too, digging into the cases that had been fought years and even decades ago, before public scrutiny was fixed on the HRCs.

Soon, the Canadian Association of Journalists put out a statement that went beyond even PEN Canada's bold release. The association said they were not only opposed to Section 13, but that they'd send in lawyers to intervene in my case and Mark Steyn's.

And then, on March 18, barely two months after my interrogation at the hands of the AHRCC, our little insurgency really hit the big time: Rick Mercer, the popular CBC political comedian, did one of his patented "rants" on the subject. Mercer opened up his commentary – watched by more than a million Canadians on the night it aired and another seven hundred thousand on its Friday rerun – with a good-humoured poke at me: "Without a doubt, he is one of the most aggravating men on this Earth," he said. I should think Shirlene McGovern of the Alberta Human Rights and Citizenship Commission wouldn't disagree. Then he told his viewers about my ordeal. "He's a freedom fighter because he has been defending his actions in front of that tribunal for the past two years," Mercer said. "He has no idea when it's gonna end, he has no right to a speedy trial, he has to pay his own legal costs, his accusers do not. Hey, it's a free country," Mercer concluded. "Well, it used to be . . . if we're not careful, if we force the Ezras in this country to shut up, our freedom of speech could be next."

Like the *Globe and Mail*'s editorial, Mercer's rant was a breakthrough. It showed that the HRCs had fallen so low that they had not only offended the most sober-minded newspaper in the country but were fodder for ridicule at the hands of a comedian on the government-owned TV network.

By the end of that month, almost every single newspaper in the country – covering all hues of the political spectrum – had come out against Canada's human rights commissions. Although these journalists were coming to the issue late, the timing actually fit the campaign quite nicely. By coincidence, just as public interest in HRCs was cresting, a major Section 13 hate speech trial was scheduled in Ottawa.

On March 25, 2008, *Warman v. Lemire* was set to resume. Lemire was going to be the first HRC defendant to get a chance to grill the commission on their use of government-made hate propaganda to entrap alleged bigots, and other procedural shenanigans. At the very moment the public was starting to pay attention to the issue, the CHRC's worst behaviour was going to be scrutinized in a public forum.

The CHRC went into lockdown mode. They had asked for a publication ban on the proceedings, and they got it. They even demanded that Lemire himself be kept out of the room while the CHRC staff testified – but that bizarre request was rejected by the chair of the hearing.

As I described earlier, the hearing was a disaster for the CHRC. Its investigators – used to being on the attack, not on the defensive – spilled the beans on everything from their online memberships in neo-Nazi groups to their use of confidential police records.

But it wasn't just *Maclean's* magazine and a few other mainstream journalists in the room: a half-dozen Ottawa-area bloggers showed up too, some of them with their own digital recorders, to tape the entire proceedings. Word of the CHRC's corrupt investigative techniques had trickled out before. In other hearings, for example, Richard Warman had admitted under oath that he had posted anti-Semitic and anti-gay comments. But there had been no reporters around. This time, there were, and they were taking notes. Especially when Bell Canada security officer Alain Monfette disclosed the name of the innocent Ottawa woman whose personal wireless computer network had been invaded by an HRC investigator to stalk Marc Lemire using a neo-Nazi identity. Reporters immediately called the woman to get her take on the story. The twenty-six-year-old was as stunned as anyone to learn that her account had been hacked – by the government, no less.

To the CHRC's collective moritification, the federal privacy commissioner launched an investigation. "Hacking into anyone else's network for your own purposes certainly seems like a breach of judgment at the very least," Colin McKay, a spokesperson for the privacy commissioner, told the Canadian Press. "We have to determine exactly what happened. It seems to be unauthorized access of the network then misrepresentation . . . If your neighbour did it to you, you'd be justifiably upset, so to have a government institution undertake that sort of activity would seem poorly considered." Within weeks, the RCMP announced that they were performing their own investigation.

The following month, the HRC sent Ian Fine, senior general counsel for the CHRC's Dispute Resolution Branch, to debate against Keith Martin and me at the Canadian Association of Journalists' annual convention – an event that would be televised nationally on CPAC, Canada's public affairs cable channel. Fine started with a written script about how the commission was just following the law, and that, in any event, most countries in the world didn't believe in full freedom of expression, so Canada shouldn't necessarily follow the "American" tradition of anything-goes free speech.

It sounded as if Fine truly didn't know that our Canadian Charter of Rights and Freedoms and Canadian Bill of Rights enshrine freedom of speech as a "fundamental freedom," and that they are part of our constitutional tradition inherited from Great Britain. In any case, since when do we give or take away freedoms based on a vote at the UN? Are China and Russia now our standard of what's right and wrong? Since when are right and wrong determined by a show of hands?

In the question-and-answer session that followed, Fine was asked for his personal views. Did he think we had too many restrictions on free speech or not enough? His response: "There can't be enough laws against hate."

The response goes to a fallacy I discussed earlier – the idea that human emotions, including hate, can be regulated by the government in the same way as drivers' licences and the price of stamps. But even if one were to accept the idea that Ottawa should be policing the emotional state of Canadian citizens, how could Fine, or anyone, credibly argue for a more bloated public apparatus in this field? Even with two hundred staff, an eight-figure budget, and a 100 per cent conviction rate for Section 13 hate speech crimes, Fine still isn't satisfied. It was a stunning moment, and it was broadcast on national television.

In the first week of June 2008, the B.C. Human Rights Tribunal went ahead with its week-long trial of *Maclean's* magazine for publishing an excerpt of Mark Steyn's book *America*

Alone. It hadn't even been five months since my videotaped interrogation, but by now the entire national press corps was on high alert. This time, the victim at centre stage was an internationally celebrated author, not the relatively unknown publisher of a small magazine. Not only was he one of Canada's most popular political satirists, but he had a massive global following, too, writing for newspapers and magazines from Thailand to Ireland, from Australia to America.

The BCHRT had never seen such public interest in one of their cases before. They decided to put three panellists on the hearing instead of the usual one. And the hearing would be chaired by the chief kangaroo herself, Heather MacNaughton. BCHRT staff also moved the hearing from their regular chambers to Vancouver's courthouse. It's unclear whether that was to accommodate a curious public or to give the hearings an air of judicial legitimacy. As it happened, only a couple of dozen reporters could squeeze in to the tiny room, which was stiflingly hot. At least fifty people waited outside the doors for a chance to go in if someone gave up their seat, but they were soon shooed away by courthouse police.

The press coverage of the hearing was brutal. The *Vancouver Sun* opined that the BCHRT was "murdering its own reputation" by even proceeding with such a farce. Even *The New York Times* flew in a reporter to cover the circus. He ran a lengthy piece comparing American respect for freedom of expression with Canadian censorship. Canada had become a laughingstock at home – and abroad. This time, there was no reluctance on the part of the news media to tackle the story. The CBC's Terry Milewski did a piece on it for *The National*, camera operators scrummed the lawyers outside the court, and bloggers blogged up a storm. *Maclean's* magazine itself sent a small army to its own hearing. In addition to three lawyers and three senior executives, they sent their national editor, Andrew Coyne, to live-blog the hearing, giving his play-by-play analysis in real time. I attended the trial for three days too, blogging my own impressions from the second row in the court room. Writing on my computer was the only way I could restrain myself from heckling the absurdities I was witnessing. My blogging from the courthouse received more than twenty thousand unique visitors a day. Andrew Coyne's blog on the larger *Maclean's* site likely had ten times as many readers. Steyn's hearing at the kangaroo court started to generate O.J. Simpson–style press coverage, minus the helicopters.

Steyn's trial electrified the grassroots fight-back campaign. But it was almost as if, instead of Steyn and *Maclean's*, it was the BCHRT and the bullies at the Canadian Islamic Congress who were on trial. As I drove back to Calgary, I heard Wally Oppal, British Columbia's Attorney General, being grilled on Vancouver's largest talk show about the circus that was going on under his watch. People weren't interested in whether Steyn was "guilty" – they wanted to know why their tax dollars were being used to stage such a totalitarian farce.

As 2008 rolled on, you could see that the human rights industry was beginning to get scared. There were a lot of oxen being gored by our campaign, and a lot of jobs and contracts at stake if our plan to reform or abolish the commissions found supporters in the offices of the prime minister and the country's premiers. About a thousand people make a pretty healthy living off of the grievance industry. Ontario's new human rights tribunal members, for example, earn $160,000 a year for a pretty slack public sector job. Each of them has 160,000 reasons to justify their kangaroo court's existence.

Most of the counterstrikes were lame, Ian Fine–style attempts at spin – the CHRC lawyer I debated on TV. But not everyone restricted themselves to words. I was hit with a spate of defamation lawsuits for criticizing the CHRC's conduct. CHRC lawyer Giacomo Vigna sued me for $50,000 for criticizing his conduct in the Lemire case. And Richard Warman, the CHRC's former employee and top customer, sued me, the *National Post*, and four other bloggers for our comments about his online impersonations. In addition to the lawsuits, I was hit with no fewer than twelve complaints to the Law Society of Alberta, as Warman, Vigna, Liberal lobbyist Warren Kinsella, and Syed Soharwardy claimed that my criticism of human rights commissions rendered me unfit to practise law. And then there was the zaniest legal threat of all: a Muslim activist from Mississauga who claimed that he had copyrighted the image of Mohammed.

Some of these nuisance suits against me have already been dismissed – and the surviving ones don't stand much chance either. But the litigants' point wasn't really to get me disbarred, or even to win a settlement. The point was to overwhelm me and the rest of the "Army of Davids" with legal hassles and bills. In January 2008, I had just the two cartoon human rights complaints against me. Six months later, I had another human rights complaint because of my anti-HRC blog, four defamation suits and notices, twelve law society complaints, and a copyright demand. That's twenty attacks. Even by human rights lawfare standards, that's a legal tidal wave.

A decade ago, these legal counterattacks would have silenced me. But that was before the blog. Every time I received a new lawsuit or human rights complaint, I immediately posted it to the Internet, so people could see for themselves that it was obviously a nuisance suit designed to shut me up. Alongside, I published a note asking my readers for help in paying my legal bills. And they responded, to the point where I was able to retain lawyers to respond to each and every action against me in the four cities in which I was sued. By the time the twelfth law society complaint was filed against me, we had what amounted to a legal assembly line ready to deal with it.

And though it's always stressful to be sued, the experience helped me understand what I was up against. It also helped me understand the anxiety and sense of siege that besets the thousands of other Canadians currently being prosecuted by the HRC and its grievance-industry allies. After years of legal torment, many CHRC victims turn sour, actually becoming the fonts of negativity the CHRC claims they are. By hiring better lawyers than the CHRC had, by staying ahead of things financially, and by venting my thoughts and feeling through my blog – with as much humour as I could muster – I made was able to avoid falling into that trap. I was determined to be a happy warrior.

Raising my spirits further was that fact that important people were now taking notice of my struggle. By the time summer 2008 came around, human rights commissions were a daily news item. An assistant to a federal cabinet minister told me that complaints about HRCs were consistently in the top two or three subjects raised by constituents in their mail to MPs.

Tellingly, the Canadian Jewish Congress (CJC) – which in recent years has been far more concerned with making nice with Muslim groups and taking good care of its friends in the human rights industry than with actually advocating Jewish interest – has started musing about "refinements" to human rights law.

B'nai Brith, which, like the CJC, has historically been a big cheerleader of human rights–mandated censorship, has come out even stronger in this regard. For the last five years, the group has been the victim of a Kafkaesque proceeding at the Manitoba Human Rights Commission, which began when complainants made vague accusations that the group had sown hatred at a 2003 conference in Winnipeg. Even by the standards of human rights prosecutions, this one is a doozy. After five years, the MHRC still has not told B'nai Brith who its accusers are, who from B'nai Brith is supposed to have said anything hateful, or what the allegedly hateful statements actually were.

"The [Manitoba] Human Rights Commission itself is supposed to be promoting human rights, but in our view in this process it's violating some pretty basic rights: a secret proceeding, a faceless accuser, failure to disclose documents," said senior B'nai Brith legal counsel David Matas in August 2008, sounding a lot like a fired-up Ezra Levant. "These are basic procedural rights being violated." (When Joseph Brean of the *National Post* called me up for a comment to include in his article on the story, I told him: "What goes around comes around. . . . It's a bit rich for [B'nai Brith] to discover their love of natural justice now.")

There was real momentum. Even the government's inaction on the HRC file started to become a mini-scandal in and of itself. The issue started to impact the Conservative Party's fundraising – with dozens of former donors diverting their political contributions to our bloggers' legal defence fund instead.

To take the pressure off the government, Rick Dykstra, a first-term MP from St. Catharines, introduced a motion to Parliament's Justice Committee calling for a complete review of the CHRC, its mandate and operations, and especially its use of Section 13 hate speech prosecutions. It was just a motion in committee, but it was a first step, and it was done with the approval of the justice minister. And if passed, it would lead to real parliamentary hearings. The awful conduct of the HRCs would be hauled into the bright lights of Parliament Hill, with the press corps assembled, with everything said under oath. Dykstra's motion was a sign that even a risk-averse minority government knew that the public landscape had changed enough that they had to act.

Even in the sleepy halls of provincial legislatures, politicians are starting to realize they've given HRCs free rein for too long. In August, for the first time ever, Ontario's Provincial Parliament held public hearings in which they interviewed new appointees for their provincial human rights tribunal – the first time any legislature in the country had been allowed to vet what is traditionally a dumping ground for political hacks and annoying activists.

It was revealing. One prospective tribunal appointee, Alan Whyte, told MPPs that if it was up to him, he'd accept human rights complaints against journalists who reported news that was discriminatory. And, of course, it will be up to him.

"If there is some sort of discrimination that comes out in the reporting that is arguably contrary to the [human rights] code, then I would also feel that it would be open to a complainant to challenge the reporting as being discriminatory on the grounds of race," he said.

Whyte didn't say what "discriminatory news" looks like. Would an article about the troubling overrepresentation of Jamaican Canadians on the Toronto police's most-wanted list count? What about a story about corruption and dysfunctionality on Native reserves? Just a few years ago, Canadians would have thought it absurd to imagine that such topics would be legally barred from their newspapers and TV news broadcasts. But the persecutions of me and Mark Steyn – as well as a dozen other related outrages – had taught them otherwise. And their disgust was beginning to show.

Chapter 9

REFORMING THE HUMAN RIGHTS COMMISSIONS, OR HOW ORDINARY CANADIANS CAN FIGHT BACK

If you've read this far, it means I've probably convinced you – at least partially – that human rights commissions, as mandated and constituted in the modern era, comprise a threat to our civil liberties. So what can ordinary Canadians do to fight back?

We've got to refuse to grant human rights mandarins the moral high ground they've come to take for granted. Civil rights activists who fought for racial equality in the 1960s deserve our honour and respect. They waged their battles in a society that truly was riven with racism, sexism, and homophobia. But times have changed. Canada now stands as a supremely tolerant and multicultural society. Women compete on an even playing field with men for jobs, racial discrimination is a huge social taboo, and gay marriage is the law of the land. Today's human rights activists who use government agencies to punish political opponents or to act out radical experiments in social engineering aren't needed any more.

As a society, we need to go back to first principles and think about the difference between real rights – such as property rights, freedom of speech, and freedom of religion – and the fake rights promoted by the HRCs, such as the made-up right not to be offended.

In short, fighting back against HRCs means taking back the language. Even small, subtle changes can be effective. At the Vancouver trial of Mark Steyn and *Maclean's*, in fact, one of the magazine's lawyers, Roger McConchie, demonstrated that changing just a single word can make a difference.

Maclean's magazine – and anyone else who is on the receiving end of an HRC complaint – is technically called a *respondent*, according to the prevailing legal jargon. But McConchie didn't use that word. This neutral, detached, legalistic term suggests a formal, objective process. It was anything but. So in describing *Maclean's* and Steyn, he instead used the word *target*. The verbal switch was subtle enough to slip by without a formal objection, but it expressed the truth that anyone unlucky enough to find themselves in an HRC's crosshairs is going to be victimized, whether they "win" their case in the end.

Even the phrase *human rights commission* is a loaded term. I've used that phrase to ensure that my readers know what I'm talking about. But in my opening remarks at my interrogation regarding the Mohammed cartoons, I told my interrogator that I'd use the words *HRC* or *the commission* because I did not want the words *human rights* tainted by association with censorship and government strong-arm tactics.

My use of the word *interrogator*, too, is a deliberate choice. Shirlene McGovern's business card said "human rights officer," and the HRC later claimed my interrogation was actually just an "interview." But why should I use those harmless-sounding words? McGovern had enormous legal powers over me, and had I resisted her "invitation" to be "interviewed," she could have ransacked my home and office. No, this was nothing less than an interrogation.

The offence with which I was charged was called discrimination. I know what discrimination means in plain English, and I didn't discriminate. That word, too, has been misappropriated.

Section 13 of the Canadian Human Rights Act also deserves a new name. As noted earlier, it's titled "hate message" in English and "hateful propaganda" in French. But Section 13 clearly isn't being used against hate messages or hateful propaganda if it's being used against Catholic priests and news magazines. Why should those targets of the HRCs accept the vocabulary of guilt? It's far more accurate to call Section 13 the thought crimes provision of the act. If you look at the wording of that law, that's what it's really about: governing the emotions and viewpoint of private citizens.

What about the various commissions and tribunals? I prefer *kangaroo courts*. (That phrase, oddly enough, seems to have originated not in Australia but in California, during the gold rush of the 1850s, where quick and dirty justice was meted out, usually without regard to the established legal norms employed out East.) I think it's a more accurate term, and it bugs the hell out of the human rights folks. I should know. Of the twelve law society complaints filed against me by people in the human rights industry, half demand that I be disciplined for using that term.

I think that Canadian judges should be leading the charge against HRCs – since the whole human rights industry trades on the generally good reputation of real courts. Canadians on the whole have a lot of respect the justice system – precisely because it is so fair. By masquerading as jurists, HRC staff dupe Canadians into according them false respect. As a result, the administration of justice everywhere is brought into disrepute.

The debate over the HRCs presents a good opportunity for Canadians to answer some very basic questions about the nature of our society. What is a right? What is a freedom? Is there a difference? The terms often are used interchangeably, but they are different. One has a right *to* something and freedom *from* something. So we have a right to life; a right to vote; a right to own property, for example. And we have rights that we create voluntarily, through contracts – and the right to sue to enforce those contracts. Freedoms are a negative right. It's the right to be left alone, really.

Upholding freedom of speech is especially important in the face of censors who purport to be acting on noble principles. After all, it's not benign speech that is at risk from censorship. No one tries to censor weather predictions or recipe books. It's the spicy stuff that needs to be safeguarded. And while we have (or are supposed to have, anyway) the freedom to speak out free from censorship, we have no right to have our views aired in someone else's magazine or TV station – or house, for that matter. Though that was exactly one of the demands placed on the *Western Standard* and *Maclean's* in the human rights complaints filed against us by Muslim radicals.

In a society such as Canada that fetishizes politeness and moderation, free speech can be hard to stomach. But that is the price we pay to live in an intellectually vibrant society that is safe for intellectual dissidents and other would-be reformers. We don't need laws to control the more reckless users – or abusers – of free speech. The community itself will naturally marginalize people who are excessively rude or bigoted. Such informal mechanisms – not Section 13 – explain why it's no longer socially acceptable to be a bigot in polite Canadian society.

The occasional rough edges that come with freedom of speech are constantly exaggerated by those who would seek to control that speech. The Canadian Jewish Congress, the Canadian Islamic Congress, B'nai Brith, and the various other shills for the human rights industry seize on every stray hateful incident to argue that the neo-Nazis will take over if we let our legislative guard down. But the trade-off they would propose – namely, having a government agency so powerful and so omnipresent in our lives as to be able to investigate, prosecute, and punish dissident ideas – is a much more troubling danger than the odd vicious comment or reactionary sermon. If the choice is between individuals using their freedom of speech hurtfully and an all-seeing Big Brother watching our words and thoughts, I know which society I'd rather live in. You can always ignore a racist. You can't escape from the government.

There is no denying that, even in the nuttiest cases, human rights commissions are trying to resolve some real underlying grievance. Beena Datt, the McDonald's employee who was let go because she couldn't wash her hands and McDonald's wouldn't accommodate her, and Kim Nixon, the male-to-female transsexual who wanted to counsel rape victims, obviously had problems with the world. Their feelings were hurt; they were offended. As a result, they'd concocted elaborate moral narratives that cast themselves as victims. Life isn't always fair or fun. But their problems just weren't real human rights complaints, and it wasn't the government's role to get involved. Not every one of life's little setbacks is something we should be running to the state to settle.

The proper response to what little bigotry is left in this society is not more government. It's the opposite: ordinary people taking a little personal responsibility when they see racism in their midst. An immediate rebuke of a racist joke by a co-worker is more effective – and more Canadian – than a five-year human rights prosecution run by a dozen government bureaucrats.

Human rights commissions are rooted in identity politics. Canadians are encouraged to look at themselves not as individuals, but as part of a particular gender or ethnic group. At an HRC, you're not a Canadian, you're a Jew or a black or a disabled person. This is the opposite of what we were brought up to do, which is to judge people on the basis of their character and actions, not irrelevant details such as skin colour. The HRCs see people as members of different groups, some of which are automatically cast in the role of victims and some of which aren't.

Identity politics quickly gives rise to grievance politics. If HRCs put you in a "victim" pigeonhole, you can sue every time someone at work does something you don't like, or a magazine publishes an article you disagree with. The kind of victimology promoted by the AHRCC's sixty thousand pamphlets to new immigrants reflects a fundamentally pessimistic view of the world. It assumes that every slight to a person's identity, no matter how minor, is of existential importance. In this worldview, citizens are encouraged to always be on the lookout for reasons to be upset – to blame others for their problems.

I've found that the best way to fight back against the HRCs is to remind Canadians what our real values are – Western values such as the rule of law, tolerance for a diversity of opinions, and freedom of speech and religion. Censorship, I like to point out, is a Saudi and Soviet value, not a Canadian one. Why should the Canadian Human Rights Commission get to call itself "Canadian" if some of the values it's promoting are North Korean imports?

Taking back the language is the first step to fighting the HRCs and denormalizing these fundamentally un-Canadian institutions. Spreading the word about their continuous stream of abusive decisions is important too. But eventually, we must get politicians involved.

A handful of politicians from various parties already have come forward, at least rhetorically, to support the reform of HRCs. In Ottawa, two dozen MPs have supported changes, ranging from a simple statement of support for Rick Dykstra's proposed parliamentary review of the CHRC, to more radical pronouncements. What's encouraging is that the movement cuts across all demographic and political lines. There are MPs from across the country, men and women, cabinet minister and backbenchers, left-wingers and right-wingers, Catholics, Protestants, Sikhs, Jews, and agnostics.

Keith Martin is one of the harshest critics of HRCs; he's compared their tactics to "pogroms." Andrew Teledgi, the Liberal MP from Kitchener-Waterloo, says he's "alarmed" by the HRCs, and feels that their power to regulate speech "infringes on those rights that we as Canadians hold so dear." Paul Szabo, the Liberal MP for Mississauga South, says he'd vote to abolish Section 13 of the CHRA and that "many MPs" share his views.

France Bonsant, the Bloc Québécois MP for Compton-Stanstead, said that her whole party was "concerned" about the HRCs' infringements on free speech, and added, "In our opinion, these commissions should not become tools for condemning legitimate opinions even if they are unpopular."

Many Conservative MPs have weighed in too. John Cummins, the MP for Delta-Richmond East, British Columbia, called on the prime minister to "weed out corruption" at the HRCs and "fight tirelessly" for free speech. James Rajotte of Edmonton Southwest said the HRCs had "overstepped their original mandates" and "must be curtailed." Bruce Stanton, the MP for Simcoe North, Ontario, called the HRCs' prosecutions "scurrilous"; Kevin Sorenson of Crowfoot, Alberta, said he had "grave concerns" with their "troubling actions"; Brad Trost from Saskatoon Humboldt called HRCs "kangaroo courts that selectively oppress Canadians."

And then there are cabinet ministers such as Jason Kenney, the minister of immigration, who's flat out called the HRCs "dangerous," and John Baird, the minister of the transport, who said he had "strong concerns" on the matter, which he would raise directly with the prime minister. The list goes on – and grows monthly. After the federal election in October, 2008, the prime minister himself weighed in on the matter. Asked by a reporter about the threat HRCs posed to free speech, Stephen Harper made a stunning announcement, all the more stunning because of his matter-of-fact tone: "In terms of the free speech issues and some of the activities of human rights commissions, I think that everyone has had some concerns about this," he said. It was an incredible comment, short-circuiting any defence of the HRCs. It wasn't even a debate: "everyone" knows HRCs are a problem, both in terms of free speech, and "some of their activities". With the CHRC, that last comment could literally mean anything from neo-Nazi publications to hacking private citizens' Internet accounts. Harper pointed out that many of the most egregious cases were in provincial HRCs, outside of this jurisdiction.

Harper didn't outline any plans for reform, but his command of the issue was a surprise. A year earlier – before the HRCs war on *Maclean's* and me, such an answer by the prime minister would have been unthinkable. And asking such a question would have been unthinkable for a reporter, too.

In November 2008, the Conservative party held their convention in Winnipeg, and voted overwhelmingly to repeal section 13 – and Rob Nicholson, the Justice Minister, publicly voted to repeal it, too. It was a non-binding test of the party's thinking on the subject, but it was a clear and hopeful sign that the federal government has noticed the issue, and is considering making changes.

There is a groundswell for reform at the provincial levels too. The persecution of Alberta's Rev. Stephen Boissoin has led that province's government to undertake an internal review of its HRC. Other provinces where official action is likely to be taken include British Columbia, because of the sheer insanity of the decisions rendered by the BCHRT and the relatively moderate ideology of the provincial Liberal government, which has already tried once to reform the system, and Saskatchewan, which has a new, open-minded provincial government under the Saskatchewan Party. Ontario, too, may reform its HRC system, though probably not immediately. It will take a couple of years before the new and adventurous mandate espoused by Chief Commissioner Barbara Hall – including subjecting news reports to a "filter" – curtails civil liberties to such an extent that Dalton McGuinty's risk-averse government is embarrassed into action.

When a government is finally ready to act, what should it do? There are two schools of thought about how to reform HRCs: prune them back or weed them out completely. Pruners think

HRCs can be salvaged – they just need to be put back in their proper place. Tweaked, not trashed.

Pruning the HRCs would likely mean removing their most abusive provisions, such as the hate speech sections. It would also mean making the procedures more fair – bringing them into synch with real courts. That would mean guarantees of speedy trials, more even-handed rules of evidence and disclosure, and a quick mechanism for rejecting nuisance complaints that obviously have no merit. Most importantly, when the target of an HRC prosecution wins, that person should be reimbursed for legal costs – preferably by the complainant.

Other common sense reforms would include a rule against double (or triple!) jeopardy, preventing complainants from filing identical complaints at many HRCs, as the Canadian Islamic Congress and its hangers-on did to *Maclean's*. Real courts typically allow plaintiffs to sue only once.

Another change that would serve to rein in HRCs would be to cap awards to a token sum. In many provinces, small claims courts only hear cases up to $10,000. If that were the limit at an HRC, it would have eliminated the case of the thin-skinned Mountie who won a staggering half-million for his claim. It's doubtful he would have spent so many years fighting if the prize had been a few thousand dollars.

Perhaps legal aid would be made available to the majority of HRC victims who are too poor to hire their own lawyer.

And the wild card played by so many HRCs – the statutory power to make unusual, even bizarre orders, such as lifetime bans on publishing websites, or orders for false apologies – might be abolished too. Those aren't allowed in real courts, because our constitution forbids "unusual" forms of punishment that are made up at the whim of the government.

Finally, pruning would likely see some of the atrocious powers granted to HRCs, especially their ability to search and seize and to compel witnesses to testify, repealed.

The attraction of the pruning approach is that it's very Canadian: it's all about compromise. The nuttier parts of the HRCs would be rolled back, but the rest would be preserved. It would be a "balanced" approach – one conceived to make noisy critics such as me go away. Certainly the one thousand government bureaucrats who make their handsome livings at Canada's fourteen HRCs would be well served by the pruning approach. If they were no longer permitted to chase down Christian or conservative websites, they'd find something equally fulfilling to do.

As for me, I'm a weeder. After reading literally hundreds of human rights commission cases from jurisdictions across the country, I've found that they all fall into one of two categories: (1) The case is a reasonable one but could have been resolved more professionally and fairly in a real court, or another government adjudicatory body; or (2) The dispute itself is simply inappropriate for government involvement altogether.

Two generations ago, racism, sexism, and homophobia were still harboured – and sometimes openly espoused – in mainstream Canadian society. But those days are over. Canadians now bend over backward to demonstrate our respect for others – both officially, through affirmative action and multiculturalism policies, and unofficially, in the way thirty-three million of us treat our friends, neighbours, and co-workers.

The CHRC "investigators" who post racist, anti-Semitic filth on Nazi webpages perfectly symbolize an obsolete industry that must sow the seeds of social disharmony in order to justify its own existence. By weeding out the HRCs, we wouldn't just save money – we would actually create a more harmonious, tolerant society.

The dozens of other boards and commissions that would fill any gaps left by the demise of the HRCs aren't just procedurally fairer. They also have a level of expertise that HRCs don't possess – and never could possess. Commissioners on labour boards or workers' compensation boards aren't judges either, and sometimes they're not even lawyers. But they often have a deep knowledge of their specific field.

It's simply impossible for members of Canada's HRCs to have specialist knowledge of all the topics they are asked to adjudicate on. One week, an HRC panellist may have to opine on restaurant hygiene and the spread of diseases; the next week, on newspapers and what can be published in them; the next, on police counterterrorism work. Their ability to evaluate this evidence is questionable. Sometimes embarrassingly so. (One only need think of the B.C. human rights panellist who ruled that McDonald's had to accommodate an employee who wasn't able to wash her hands as often as her employer wished.)

If Canada needs any sort of human rights commission, it needs the kind that would buttress our real human rights by inculcating our Western, liberal values into new immigrants, many of whom come to Canada from cultures where men and women aren't treated equally, where institutional violence is used to solve problems, where ethnic groups and castes live in a perpetual state of segregation and hostility, and where religious minorities are vilified.

Few schools teach civics in a formal way – to immigrant or Canadian-born kids. And adult immigrants may have very little exposure to our Western values at all, since Canada's official citizenship brochures and even the citizenship test are almost entirely silent on the subject. A new breed of HRC might change this by working with education ministries and school boards to create courses and public education campaigns aimed at instilling newcomers with our most sacrosanct liberal values – including freedom of speech. In fact, we might all benefit from studying the Charter of Rights and Freedoms of 1982 and the Bill of Rights, introduced by John Diefenbaker nearly fifty years ago.

There are always dangers involved when you let the government into the civic education business; such projects are ripe for political hijacking by interest groups, and other forms of abuse. But if there really is a need for the promotion of human rights, wouldn't a reiteration of fundamental rights, the building blocks of our Western tradition, be more useful than the human rights commissions we have now?

There is another, radical option for reforming the HRCs – one that some believe may become necessary if the methods I've outlined above don't bear fruit. It would involve the "Army of Davids" engaging in the ultimate act of anti-HRC civil disobedience: to overwhelm the human rights commissions by filing thousands of complaints, against every single person who has ever filed a human rights complaint. Why not? It's free to you and me. You don't even need a stamp; just fax in your complaint form and let taxpayers do the rest. These wouldn't be baseless complaints. In any event no more baseless than the kind of complaints discussed in this book. And there's no risk if you fail; the target still has to spend time and money fighting it.

Under this radical option, the Canadian Islamic Congress, which complained about *Maclean's* magazine and Mark Steyn, would be hit with complaints that it is anti-Semitic. So would

Syed Soharwardy and the Edmonton Council of Muslim Communities, which filed complaints against the *Western Standard.*

All the radical gay activists who filed complaints against Christian clergy could be targeted for payback too – they've surely uttered anti-religious comments. (Rob Wells, a serial human rights complainant against priests and pastors, actually drives around Edmonton in a vehicle plastered with stickers comparing Christians to Nazis; for three months, he had an anti-Catholic vigil outside a church, harassing congregants as they went in and out).

And how about lodging complaints against anyone who has supported human rights commissions in the recent national debate? There haven't been many. But *Toronto Star* columnist Haroon Siddiqui and *Calgary Herald* columnist Naomi Lakritz both have explicitly defended government censorship. Abraham Lincoln once said that whenever he heard someone defending slavery, he had half a mind to see it tried out on them. Lots of people feel the same way about journalists who support censorship for others. Why not give them that experience, first-hand?

Of course, there are the human rights commissions themselves. The CHRC's anti-hate squad has published hundreds of bigoted comments online. Why not charge all of them too?

And with fourteen human rights commissions in Canada from Newfoundland to Nunavut, why not put each target through fourteen different trials?

If only fifty activists signed on to such a campaign, and each activist targeted twenty people or organizations, that's a thousand complaints – fourteen times over. Given the number of recruits the "Army of Davids" has attracted since the beginning of 2008, it should be easy to get a lot more than fifty activists involved in the campaign. All things considered, it really wouldn't be too much hassle to file ten thousand complaints, or perhaps even one hundred thousand, nationwide.

Just imagine: one hundred thousand new human rights complaints, over the course of a month, targeting public figures, lobby groups, and political activists, all of whom have publicly supported HRCs, none of whom ever thought they'd be targets themselves. And they probably wouldn't like it much. B'nai Brith Canada, an active user of Section 13, put out a squawking press release when it was tagged with a hate speech charge for organizing a counterterrorism conference in Winnipeg after 9/11. A local Muslim activist who didn't even attend the conference claimed it was anti-Muslim, and the B'nai Brith has been on the defensive ever since. Imagine if every pro-HRC group had the same legal perversion inflicted on them, from tens of different complainants.

Imagine the time it would take. Not for the complainants. For the targets. And for the HRC bureaucrats, who would be tied up just processing all that paper. Why, the CHRC might even have to divert staff away from their important work posting hate speech on Nazi websites.

At the same time, it would be a huge, national teaching moment: Freedom's enemies would be taught, first-hand, what it's like to be caught in the flypaper of such a Kafkaesque system. It would be a circus too, of course – but an educational circus, in which the flaws of the HRC system would be exposed for the national media's delight and ridicule.

This idea of flooding the HRCs with complaints has been bruited a lot on the Internet. Dean Skoreyko of Coldstream, British Columbia, decided to do give it a try, at least on a small scale. Skoreyko got the notion from a stunt he saw on the

Showcase television program *Kenny vs. Spenny*, in which two comedians enter into strange contests with each other. In one particular 2008 episode, the two men competed to see who could offend more people. Kenny – Kenneth Hotz – hired an airplane to pull a banner across Toronto with the words *Jesus sucks* trailing behind it. Funny? Not really. Daring? Not really. Poking fun at Christians is so banal we barely even notice it any more.

But Skoreyko noticed. And he filed a complaint with the B.C. Human Rights Tribunal. (The fact that the stunt took place in Toronto didn't stop him – the show airs across the country.) Skoreyko probably knows he won't win. In thirty years, not a single HRC case has ever gone to trial where the target has been accused of anti-Christian hate speech. But he also knows it will cost the producers of *Kenny vs. Spenny* a lot of time and money. And in any case, he is making a point about the manner in which people abuse the HRC system. His complaint took less than five minutes to fill out – but it will cause months, or even years, of hassles for a bunch of TV industry staffers and their lawyers.

The analogy with my own protest concept isn't perfect: Kenny and Spenny are politically incorrect media personalities – hardly the sort of sanctimonious scolds who trumpet for human rights commissions. But the gesture will at least have the virtue of highlighting the HRCs' left-wing bias: if the BCHRT rejects Skoreyko's claim – which they likely will – it will come as yet more proof that HRCs apply the law arbitrarily: you can bet that if the "Jesus" of the banner had instead been Mohammed, Moses, Martin Luther King, or Guru Nanak, the result would be very different.

Ultimately, though, I've concluded that this denial of service–style approach to fighting the HRCs is a bad idea. Smacking the commissions' defenders with thousands of complaints sounds exciting and deliciously mischievous. It would have the taste of vengeance. But it would also be unprincipled. By using the HRCs' immoral system – even as a gesture of protest – we would be implicitly legitimizing it. Moreover, it is easy to imagine the HRCs turning such a stunt to their advantage – citing the increased number of human rights complaints as proof that human rights infractions are on the rise, and that the commissions need new funding, new staff, and – if Ian Fine had his way – plenty more laws.

These kangaroo courts ought to be fought in the court of public opinion, in the court of law if necessary, and in Parliament. There's no need to give tacit approval to the bullying tactics we need to excise. Instead, we should devote our efforts to a sustained campaign that exposes the appalling reality of the HRCs. This book represents part of my contribution to this important campaign. You can read more about my ongoing efforts at EzraLevant.com.

If you find the case I've made persuasive, I urge you to join me in this important fight. Speak your mind now. If you don't do it today, by the time tomorrow comes, it just may be illegal.

ACKNOWLEDGEMENTS

This battle began in the pages of the *Western Standard* magazine, and though that magazine is gone, part of its legacy is the fight for freedom this book describes. I'd like to thank everyone involved in that project, from our investors to our staff and readers. Since my government interrogation in January 2008, my campaign for reform – and my enormous legal bills – have been supported by hundreds of people across Canada and around the world. I'm grateful to them for their faith and generosity.

I'd like to thank the people who made this book possible. My editor and friend, Jonathan Kay; Doug Pepper and his team at McClelland & Stewart, including the very patient Jenny Bradshaw; and my agent Michael Levine.

Finally, I'd like to thank my friend Mark Steyn, not only for his generous introduction to the book, but for being such an eloquent advocate for freedom, and such a generous supporter of my own personal battle.

Appendix A

FORTY-SIX QUESTIONS AND PROFESSOR RICHARD MOON

The Canadian Human Rights Commission is under attack – not just from amateur bloggers and political activists, but from professionals, too. The disastrous March, 2008 human rights tribunal hearing in the *Warman v. Lemire* case, which revealed some of the CHRC's bizarre investigative practices, sparked no fewer than four investigations into the CHRC's conduct.

Canada's Privacy Commissioner was the first to act, followed quickly by the RCMP. Both focused on the revelation that the CHRC accessed the Internet, while in their neo-Nazi personas, through the wireless Internet network of a private citizen. Next came the Parliamentary investigation proposed by Rick Dykstra, a Conservative MP on the Justice Committee, who proposed Parliamentary hearings into the Section 13 hate speech provision of the Human Rights Act, as well as the CHRC's operational irregularities.

Faced with this battery of investigations – and the bad press being generated – the CHRC launched an "investigation" of its own. Jennifer Lynch, the CHRC's chief commissioner, handpicked a university professor to do a "review" of the CHRC himself, and to report back to her directly.

Professor Richard Moon of the University of Windsor was Ms. Lynch's choice, and no wonder: Moon had published a book about freedom of expression, in which he came out in favour of the government's power to "open up the media to a wider range of voices and views" – which I interpret as meaning, to override editors' decisions about what they could or could not publish. That's exactly the kind of power that the Canadian Islamic Congress demanded the CHRC exercise against *Maclean's*.

Of course, there's something obviously wrong with a bureaucrat hiring someone to "investigate" herself. There's an appearance of a conflict of interest, since Moon's review was mandated and funded by Lynch herself – to the tune of $1,000/page. Worse, since it was going on at the same time as the three other independent inquiries – and will likely conclude before they do – Moon's review was clearly a public relations exercise.

The plan was transparent: when Moon was done, his carefully-limited review would surely vindicate Lynch and her agency, whether or not the other investigations did.

Not surprisingly, Lynch's decision to appoint someone to investigate her while she's already the subject of a proposed Parliamentary review was met with derision on Parliament Hill by the CHRC's critics. The CHRC is a creation of Parliament, is funded by Parliament and answers to it. For the CHRC to decide, on its own, that it would hire someone to review its own mandate and purpose was an act of unbridled arrogance by civil servants who seemed to fancy themselves unelected politicians.

If Parliament didn't give the CHRC's pre-emptive self-examination much credence, why would I? Other amateur critics of the CHRC – and a few supporters – lined up to give Moon their views. I hesitated: If I participated in what I thought was an illegitimate procedure, wasn't I legitimizing it? If I tried to persuade Moon of my views on freedom of speech, wasn't I implying that I thought he – or the CHRC, or anyone – had some sort of moral authority in the first place?

Ultimately, I decided that if the CHRC was going to use Moon for their propaganda purposes, I should too. I immediately wrote to the professor, and asked him if I could make a submission to him. He told me that he had been following my blog, and knew of my general concerns, but that I was welcome to send him a formal submission. So I did.

Below is my submission. It wasn't an attempt to persuade him of anything. Rather, it was an attempt to put prickly questions about the CHRC on the public record, to show the kind of questions that a real inquiry ought to ask, and to shame the CHRC when they refuse to answer them.

From asking Moon how much he was paid for his review, to asking about the CHRC's use of neo-Nazi personas, there were 46 uncomfortable questions. Moon wrote back to me immediately in an e-mail (included below) asserting his independence but ruling out any answers about key CHRC problems under police investigation.

But to my great shock – and Lynch's as well – Moon defied expectations. His report recommended that Section be scrapped, ending the CHRC's mandate to investigate hate speech. It was a stunning rebuke of the CHRC, all the more so since it came from a CHRC consultant.

To be sure, there were still plenty of flaws in Moon's report. He called for other tools of censorship, like a mandatory "press council" that had the power to order newspapers to run or not run certain things – basically a human rights commission just for the press. And there were other weird ideas in there, too. But all of that was irrelevant. Moon's report was never about anything more than public relations, and the headlines across the country the next day blared his findings: repeal section 13.

Lynch must have been apoplectic – and it showed. In the CHRC's official press release announcing Moon's report, nowhere was the world "repeal" mentioned, though his report contained that word eleven times. Lynch immediately announced that there would be more consultations, a sudden change of plans that was as transparent as it was clumsy: Lynch was obviously going to keep asking the same question until she got the answer she wanted. Moon was just a very expensive mistake for her.

Here are the 46 questions I sent to Moon. By the way, in the end he ended up answering not a single one of them. We'll have to wait for the police, or Parliament, or a forensic auditor, to answer these.

Dear Prof. Moon,

Further to your e-mail, below please find my submission to your review. It is in the form of a list of questions. Should you need any primary documents referred to in the questions, I would be happy to send them to you; most of them can be found on my blog.

There are many more questions in similar veins. I'm limiting my submission to these few, as I doubt that your report will – or will be allowed to – address them in a meaningful way.

I believe that your review is merely a political smokescreen, a placebo to pretend that the CHRC is accountable, when in fact it has hand-picked you, has limited the scope of your work, and has done so to pre-empt an RCMP investigation, a Privacy Commissioner investigation and a nascent Parliamentary review.

Frankly, I expect that few of my questions will be answered in your report. I hope that I'm wrong; but if not, I will surely pass on my list of questions to the Parliamentary review – the one that the CHRC answers to, not the one that answers to the CHRC.

Yours truly,

Ezra Levant

Procedural details about your review

1. Other than the published terms of reference of your review, have you received any other instructions, in writing, verbally, or in any other form, from the CHRC or anyone else? If so, what are those instructions?
2. Have you been instructed that there are certain issues that you are not to discuss?
3. Have you had any interim meetings with Jennifer Lynch, or any other CHRC staff, or others, during which you have been asked about the status of your work, or been given feedback or direction on your work to date, or otherwise received instructions?
4. Have you received any instructions, advice or input from the CHRC's public relations or government relations staff or contractors?
5. Will anyone see your report prior to its final publication? Will it be reviewed, edited or embargoed by the CHRC prior to its release? Will you release it, or will the CHRC?
6. Have you been granted access to CHRC records, including computer files, internal memoranda, meeting minutes or any other CHRC resources? Have you been granted authority to interview CHRC staff, or former staff? Did you do so?

7. What compensation will you receive for your review? Have you been promised any other future consideration?

Inappropriateness of the CHRC reviewing Parliament's mandate

8. Under what authority is the CHRC reviewing the mandate given to it by Parliament? What statutory or regulatory provision authorizes the CHRC to second-guess its standing orders given to it by the elected legislature?
9. Who, if anyone, did the CHRC consult prior to its announcement of your review? Did it consult MPs? The PMO or PCO? The Justice Minister? Any public relations or government relations staff or contractors?

Other contemporaneous reviews

10. Were you instructed to avoid reviewing the matters currently being investigated by the RCMP and the Privacy Commissioner into the unauthorized access of a private citizen's Internet account by CHRC staff?
11. What is the status of those investigations? What CHRC staff, former staff, contractors or former contractors have been interviewed?
12. Have any search warrants been issued relating to CHRC records or other property such as hard drives? Have the CHRC offices been searched? Has anything been seized?
13. Were the actions being investigated done in the course of CHRC duties? Who approved those actions?
14. Has the CHRC paid for criminal lawyers for those being investigated? Who has been investigated so far?
15. Has the CHRC made any offer of a settlement to Nelly Hechme?

CHRC investigative tactics that spread hate

16. What is the CHRC policy on impersonation and entrapment by CHRC investigators and other officers? Is there a policy? Who wrote it? Has it been promulgated to the staff?
17. What is the CHRC policy regarding CHRC staff committing section 13 hate speech offences while impersonating neo-Nazis or other bigots? Is there a policy? Who wrote it? Has it been promulgated to the staff?
18. Does the CHRC continue to use false personas?

CHRC lack of ethics code

19. In a recent internal governance audit, the CHRC received a failing grade for ethics, and was found not to have a code of ethics. Since that time, has the CHRC adopted an ethics code?
20. If so, what is it? How is that ethics code being implemented? What operational changes, if any, have resulted from that? What are the penalties, if any, for violating ethical norms?
21. What ethical standards, if any, does the CHRC use to screen candidates for employment? Is it appropriate that a former police officer who was drummed out of the force for corruption works as an investigator at the CHRC?

Improper investigation of political websites

22. The CHRC has admitted to investigating political websites, such as Free Dominion, even in the absence of any complaint. What political websites is the CHRC currently investigating?
23. What is the CHRC policy about investigating websites before a complaint is made? If that policy prohibits such

investigations, has that policy been enforced, and have CHRC staff been disciplined or otherwise corrected?

24. Does the CHRC have any oversight committee, or even a single manager, who ensures that CHRC investigators do not engage in personal political vendettas?

CHRC improper use of police powers, evidence

25. The CHRC regularly asks Canadian police forces (and CSIS) for information and evidence to which the CHRC is not statutorily entitled, including evidence seized by police pursuant to criminal search warrants, where the CHRC's interest is not disclosed; access to the CPIC police database; and police and CSIS surveillance. What is the CHRC's policy regarding evidence acquired in this manner? Who drafted this policy?
26. Has this policy been approved by any judicial review? Has it been disclosed to the police departments' respective oversight bodies? Has it been disclosed to Parliament?

Richard Warman

27. Richard Warman was a CHRC employee from 2002 to 2004. While he was at the CHRC, he began filing section 13 hate speech complaints that were reviewed by his colleagues. He has continued to do so since he left. He has filed half of all complaints, and 12 out of 14 cases that have gone to the CHRT over the past five years have been Warman's complaints. The CHRC calls Warman as their witness in his own complaints, thus enabling them to pay his expenses for being a witness in his own complaints. Does Warman have any status with the CHRC whatsoever, other than as a complainant?

28. Does the CHRC have any policy regarding the conflict of interest of having current or former staffers file CHRC complaints?
29. Does Warman have any access to CHRC offices, e-mail accounts, computer files, passwords or Internet aliases such as Jadewarr? When was that access cut off?
30. What compensation does Warman continue to receive from the CHRC? Does he have any ongoing contracts with the CHRC? When he appears as a witness for the CHRC, does he receive any fee whatsoever, including a per diem payment? What are those payments? Do any other CHRC complainants receive them?
31. Warman's use of false identities to entrap CHRC respondents has been criticized by the CHRT. What review, if any, has the CHRC done of Warman's tactics? Have they made any policy changes in response to the CHRT 's criticisms?
32. Section 13 hate speech complaints filed against Warman for his bigoted posts have been rejected by the CHRC, despite an investigator's assessment that Warman did in fact breach section 13. Why are CHRC staff and former staff exempt from section 13 hate speech investigations?

CHRC lack of respect for Charter values

33. Dean Steacy, the senior section 13 hate speech investigator for the CHRC, testified that "freedom of speech is an American concept, so I don't give it any value . . . It's not my job to give value to an American concept." Does Steacy's testimony represent the CHRC's view of freedom of speech?
34. If not, what is the CHRC's view of freedom of speech? Has that view been promulgated within the organization? Has Steacy been corrected in his view or disciplined? How?

35. If the CHRC has changed its view, or if Steacy's view was a rogue view, have there been any changes to the way that Steacy and other section 13 hate speech staff operate?
36. Will the CHRC publicly state its new policy regarding freedom of speech to contradict the impression left by Steacy?

CHRC failure to comply with natural justice

37. The CHRC regularly refuses to comply with rules of natural justice, and even its own rules of procedure. On what legal basis does the CHRC redact its disclosure, contrary to its rules of procedure, as in the Lemire case? On what legal basis does the CHRC disclose documents after the hearings have begun, as in the Lemire case? At what level of the CHRC has this process been approved?
38. The Information Commissioner has recently ruled that the CHRC is in violation of its access to information obligations. What changes, if any, has the CHRC made to comply with the law?
39. In the recent Lemire hearing of March 25, 2008, the CHRC made a transcript of the hearing, but did not disclose it to the respondent, despite his requests – but sent it to journalists. Who approved this decision? Is it standard CHRC policy to withhold transcripts from respondents?
40. That transcript was found to have been inaccurate in a substantial manner that would have disadvantaged the respondent. Was that transcript edited at the instruction of the CHRC?
41. The CHRC regularly calls for publication bans; withholds evidence; and has even applied for a respondent to be physically barred from the hearing room during parts of his own hearing. In one case, the identity of a complainant was

withheld from the respondent by the CHRC. Who approves these abusive legal tactics? Is there a CHRC legal procedural manual?

42. 91% of the CHRC's section 13 hate speech targets are too poor to hire lawyers. Why is it acceptable to the CHRC to prosecute people who are unrepresented by competent counsel, without providing them with legal aid?

Improper political influence

43. The B'nai Brith and the Canadian Jewish Congress, two groups that are parties or intervenors in support of CHRC complaints, are registered lobbyist targeting the CHRT. What was the CHRC's involvement with this lobbying? Is it appropriate for parties before the CHRT to lobby the CHRT ex parte? Are there any other quasi-judicial tribunals in which such explicit attempts to influence decision-making are considered legal?

44. The CHRC has never prosecuted a section 13 hate speech complaint against a Canadian from a minority background – 100% have been white. This is odd, given that there is evident "hate speech" within various ethnic minorities in Canada including, just to name a few, from Tamil, Sikh, Muslim and other immigrant communities, including amongst those communities, between radical and moderate elements. Does the CHRC have a policy to only prosecute white hate speech cases? If not, why have no other prosecutions been made?

CHRC bullying of its critics

45. In response to my criticism of the CHRC's conduct, I have been sued in civil court by a CHRC lawyer, Giacomo Vigna, specifically for criticizing his work as a CHRC lawyer. Vigna

has threatened me with a second lawsuit. He has also filed seven law society complaints against me – all for my criticism of his conduct with the CHRC, or of the CHRC in general. Does the CHRC have a policy regarding lawsuits by staff against CHRC critics?

46. Were CHRC managers or staff aware of Vigna's lawsuit before it was filed? If so, what feedback was Vigna given as to the appropriateness of a lawsuit being filed against a political critic of the CHRC?

Those are my submissions.

Moon wrote back to me right away, with the following reply:

Mr. Levant: My instructions from the CHRC are contained in the mandate that is posted on the CHRC website. No one connected with the CHRC has asked me to do anything more or less than that. I can assure you that this will be an independent report. You may agree or disagree with my recommendations but they will be my recommendations.

I will not be considering allegations of illegal behaviour on the part of the CHRC staff. I have neither the authority, nor the expertise, to engage in such an investigation. I will, however, be examining the CHRC investigation process.

Your substantive questions, I will hope to address in the report itself.

best wishes

Richard Moon
Professor of Law

Appendix B
INSIDE STORMFRONT.ORG

There are a lot of side streets and dead ends on the information superhighway. A particularly rough stretch of road is a neo-Nazi website called Stormfront.org.

Stormfront is based in West Palm Beach, Florida, and not just because most of its online members are from the United States: The site's high-octane racism would likely get it shut down in a hurry in countries without a strong commitment to freedom of speech.

Just clicking on the site's home page is shocking. The motto is "white pride world wide," and the featured hero is former Ku Klux Klan grand dragon David Duke. Another website, the Vanguard News Network (VNN), features even rougher stuff. It's based in Kirksville, Missouri.

Neither calls itself a Nazi site; they prefer the phrase *white nationalist*. But there's not much difference: Many members of the sites choose Internet nicknames that pay homage to Adolf Hitler, or use Nazi shorthand such as AH, for Adolf Hitler, and

88 – "h" being the eighth letter of the alphabet, 88 standing for "Heil Hitler."

I've spent a fair amount of time surfing Stormfront and VNN. Obviously, that's not because I agree with the hateful opinions on display. Rather, I think that enemies of censorship have an intellectual responsibility to acquaint themselves with the ugly side of free speech. We need to acknowledge that some people will use their right to free expression to advance the most appalling views imaginable.

My impression of Stormfront and VNN is that they constitute a very weird online world: part bigoted propaganda, part fantasy dress-up party. Anonymous members from around the world join the websites under pseudonyms and choose a picture that represents them. As you'd expect, the men who join these sites – and it's about 99 per cent men – typically choose macho images of Aryans, Nazis, or medieval knights. It's like an Internet dating site, but instead of everybody pretending to be a little more attractive than they are, everybody on these sites is pretending to be more dangerous and nutty.

The sites feature blogs and Internet radio stations, but the main area of activity is the chat sites, where members can weigh in on everything from politics to history to archeology – all coloured with the white-pride theme. (There's even a Vanguard forum about corned beef – which inevitably degenerated into anti-Semitic gibes against kosher food.)

It's a world inhabited by fantasists who either wish they were around during what they consider to be the glory years of the Third Reich or who harbour delusional dreams that North America is on the verge of a white uprising against Jews, Blacks, gays, and other minorities. A lot of it seems animated by deep-seated macho insecurity: many of the participants love pretending they're tough Aryans who would have led a Panzer division had they been around seventy years ago.

In a way, the existence of Stormfront and Vanguard is a testament to how marginalized racism has become: The only place it's acceptable is in marginalized online playpens, where the epithets are shouted anonymously into cyberspace by delusional cranks.

But, as documented earlier, some of the busiest propagators of racism on those sites are actually human rights officers, looking to entrap Canadians under the Canadian Human Rights Act's Section 13 hate speech law. In fact, much of my time on Stormfront and VNN has been spent researching the anti-Semitic, anti-Black, and anti-gay comments posted there by CHRC staff with pseudonyms such as Axetogrind and Pogue Mahone.

Even knowing that many of the haters on the site are government moles, it's still creepy to see people quoting the likes of Joseph Goebbels – Adolf Hitler's propaganda minister. Spending more than a few minutes on the site is numbing – there is so much vileness, one starts to become desensitized to it. Typically, political analysis consists of blaming the Jews or Blacks for any misfortune, and calling any political enemy a Jew, whether he or she is or not.

What's heartening, though, is that these folks are pretty much all talk. There is occasional chatter on the websites about a white pride march somewhere (which usually ends up drawing a few dozen fanatics, half of whom are police infiltrators). But mainly, the sites attract society's layabouts, blowing off steam with other layabouts. What looks at first like a terrifying collection of SS troopers is really just a scattered convention of homebody bigots.

The irony, of course, is that many of the folks fighting for the free-speech rights of these anti-Semites are Jews such as me.

The bigots on VNN and Stormfront are unsure how to deal with that fact. It just doesn't compute.

"Not every single Jew on planet earth is bad, some do good things," wrote "Bill," who had 3,746 anti-Semitic comments to his credit on VNN. "F.W. Braun," who calls himself a "blondist," agreed, saying that I had "more guts than 95% of posters [on the Vanguard site]." That's quite a statement from someone who signs his online comments with a quote from Joseph Goebbels to the effect that "opposing Jews is a matter of personal hygiene."

Unfortunately, "Alex Linder," the site's administrator, wouldn't tolerate such deviance. "There's no bravery involved at all," he wrote. "[Levant] relies on his jewiness for protection." (I confess it: My Jewiness is like a forcefield!)

When Jonathan Kay, a Jewish editor at the *National Post*, wrote a February 2008 column condemning the CHRC's censorship, Linder started a discussion about it, called "More Jewing about Free Speech in Canada."

"The only time jews come out in favor of free speech is when laws against it are used against jews," he wrote. "I swear god, you cannot find a single article about free speech in Canada, published in a major paper, that was not written by a kike." (It's hard to understand Linder's point: He seems frustrated that Jews don't defend free speech enough, but then points out that many of the arguments for free speech are in fact written by Jews. Then again, anti-Semitic conspiracy theorists aren't exactly known for the rigor of their logic.)

"Keepitanonymous" on Stormfront had the perfectly incoherent conspiracy theory to answer Linder's incoherent riddle: "you really know canada is run by jews when you have jews fighting on both sides of an issue like this."

"Kufenstecher" had a more straightforward argument. Writing

about Mark Steyn (who is non-Jewish) and me, he said, "Having seen photos of the pair and having some rough biographical information on them, I think it's permissible to have a basic aversion to them simply because they are jews."

"I suppose if Levant and Steyn want to be traitors to their own Jewish race there's no reason for us to discourage them," concluded "Folkwise," a Stormfront member who preferred to look at the bright side of things.

"Anyone who hates them simply because they are jews, or is unable to engage with them on issues of common interest simply because they are Jews, is irrational, and beneath us," agreed "Yehuda Abraham," an anti-Semite who chose a curiously semitic Internet nickname.

"So much for AH!" replied Folkwise – referring to Adolf Hitler.

And on it went.

It's odd reading the thoughts of skinheads, racists and other misfits. It's pitiful, actually. These are sad, grotesque minds. But these people are not criminals – or they ought not to be. Yet these specimens are the traditional target of HRCs. Indeed, the majority of the CHRC's Section 13 cases have been prosecuted against uneducated, poor white supremacists. (By one accounting, 91 per cent of Section 13 defendants couldn't even afford a lawyer.)

These people should be protected from censorship not because they're right about the world. They're very, very wrong. They should be protected from injustice because we believe in right and wrong, even if they don't. It's wrong to criminalize bad ideas, even racist ideas. That's why I'm supporting freedom of speech. Not for the white trash on Stormfront and Vanguard – but despite them.

Appendix C

THE THIRD COMPLAINT, WELLS V. LEVANT

If there were any doubt that human rights complaints long ago ceased to be about real civil rights issues, and have now become little more than political weapons, the case of *Rob Wells v. Ezra Levant* should put the matter to rest.

That's the name of the third human rights complaint filed against me; and it probably won't be the last. (Prediction: this book itself will yield at least one complaint!)

I've never met Rob Wells. I'd never even heard of him until I started researching the political abuses of Section 13 of the Canadian Human Rights Act, the hate speech provision. That's when I discovered Wells. He's an Edmonton gay rights activist who's made complaining against Christians something of a hobby. He's filed human rights complaints against Fr. Alphonse de Valk, the Toronto publisher of *Catholic Insight* magazine, the Christian Heritage Party, and Craig Chandler, a Christian political activist in Alberta.

Wells obviously has a problem with the Christian view on gay rights, and that's his right in a free society. He's even free to be rude about it – which he is. As mentioned in the last chapter, Wells set up a lengthy one-man anti-Catholic vigil outside Edmonton's St. Joseph's Basilica, holding up signs insulting churchgoers as they came and went. He created a hate-mobile, which he'd drive around brandishing anti-Catholic signs.

Catholics weren't his only target. During an election campaign, Wells proudly drove the streets with a "Fuck Harper" bumper sticker, sharing his deep thoughts on political philosophy with everyone else on the road, from little grannies to school buses full of children.

You'd think that such a foul-mouthed troublemaker would be a free speech aficionado himself. And you'd be correct – when it comes to his own right to insult. But when Wells's opponents exercise their freedom of speech and religion, in much more moderate ways, he's quick to file complaints to the nearest HRC. Even when he loses – as he did with *Catholic Insight* – he still wins: He's not out a dime, yet he's dragged one of his enemies through the mud for months, and cost them tens of thousands of dollars in legal fees.

Which is how I found myself in Wells's crosshairs. In June 2008, I was writing about the outlandish punishments meted out by Alberta's human rights commission against Rev. Stephen Boissoin for publishing an editorial critical of gay marriage. As noted earlier, the original complaint had been filed by Darren Lund, an even crankier anti-Christian activist. But Wells piled on, filing an identical complaint with the national HRC – which promptly found Reverend Boissoin to have broken their law too.

It was a classic case of legal abuse of process. Neither Lund nor Wells had been personally affected by Reverend Boissoin, but they both were given standing by HRCs to complain. Such double jeopardy would be illegal in any real court.

I was talking up a storm about Reverend Boissoin's case, on my blog, on talk radio, and even in the pages of the *National Post*. As part of my argument, I published Reverend Boissoin's original editorial – the one that had got him into hot water in the first place.

I wasn't the only person to publish Reverend Boissoin's words. The *Red Deer Advocate* newspaper had done so in the first place. So did a gay newspaper called *Xtra*, which obviously didn't agree with it. I jumped in too – not just so that readers could see how low the bar had fallen for what constitutes a hate crime, but as a symbolic expression of my own freedom, and my disdain for the Alberta HRC's conviction of Reverend Boissoin.

That's when Wells made his move: He filed a complaint against me for republishing Reverend Boissoin's editorial on my website. The CHRC promptly launched an investigation.

But Wells's timing was off. By the time he sued me, the cartoon complaints against me were already big news, and the human rights trial of *Maclean's* magazine for publishing Mark Steyn's book excerpt was also a front-page item. Politicians were taking notice and wondering what political score-settling had to do with the original civil rights mandate of HRCs. The last thing the CHRC needed was to pick another fight with me, a point-man in the freedom-of-speech battle.

So they didn't. On August 8, the CHRC sent a letter to Rob Wells, and copied it to me, advising him that they weren't going to proceed any further with his complaint.

It was actually the first I'd heard of the complaint – they hadn't sent me a copy of Wells's complaint or advised me in any way when he first filed the thing. It was only when they were moving to dismiss it that they let me in on the fact that I had been thoroughly investigated for nearly two months.

Even then, the letter was signed illegibly – no-one from the CHRC would put their name to it.

I can understand why. Had they done what they were supposed to do – let me know I was the subject of a complaint, and under government investigation – I would have launched a public relations war against them, just as I had with the cartoon complaints. By keeping me in the dark until they were going to throw the complaint out, they saved themselves two months of daily embarrassment. Damage control had become job one at the CHRC.

Normally, I'd be happy to know that the CHRC had the wits to reject a complaint against me for publishing mere words on a website. In this case, though, I couldn't help but ask: Why had I been excused for committing the exact same word crime for which Reverend Boissoin was convicted and punished?

Why was I free to go, while Reverend Boissoin was not? Why was the decision in my case made in two months, but in Reverend Boissoin's case, he was dragged through nearly six years of grinding procedures?

These questions were easy to answer because the contrast between the two complaints comprised a perfect scientific experiment – with all important conditions the same except for one: the main difference between Reverend Boissoin's case and mine was that I was a noisy, feisty Jew with a legal defence fund and he was a Christian pastor who didn't have strong public relations skills. We both published the exact same words – I reprinted his original editorial, literally word for word. The only factor that was different was the identity of the publisher.

Actually, what I had done was arguably *worse* from the point of view of an HRC. Reverend Boissoin was a Christian pastor, writing words he deeply and truly believed. I was just reprinting his words – gay marriage really isn't a big issue for me, as it was for him. His publication of the words was a reflection of his deep faith; my publication of them was just to prove a point.

And when Reverend Boissoin wrote those words, he did so thinking they were perfectly legitimate – the thought that, six years later, he'd be convicted of "hate speech" never crossed his mind. I, on the other hand, knew full well that the words had been deemed illegal by the government of Alberta, and I proceeded to republish them nonetheless.

Reverend Boissoin was speaking from his heart, in good faith. I was causing trouble. Yet he was the one punished. I was given a free pass. Why?

In their eighteen-page letter to me explaining why they were dismissing Wells's complaint, the CHRC devoted a brief passage to explaining their double standard. "The letter appeared in a different context," they wrote.

The CHRC explained that I was let go because my website – where I had published Reverend Boissoin's words – wasn't a "forum which espouses extreme views of hatred." But, then, neither was the *Red Deer Advocate*, that city's newspaper of record, where Reverend Boissoin himself published the same material.

The CHRC said my publication was "more likely" to promote a debate about free speech than to spread hatred. But Reverend Boissoin's case has sparked a six-year debate, and one that will continue until the clearly unconstitutional penalties foisted upon him are overturned by a real court. So that explanation rings hollow as well.

Even if it were true that I was a better debater than Reverend Boissoin, what's that got to do with the law? Section 13 of the Canadian Human Rights Act has no defence for people who spark a debate. Even the CHRC's most odious targets – Holocaust-denying neo-Nazis – spark a debate, or try to. The cases of such notorious specimens as James Keegstra and Ernst Zündel are debated in law school classrooms to this day – yet no one claims their convictions should be overturned on that basis.

That's the thing about Section 13: It's focused 100 per cent on words, not on criminal deeds. *Everyone* charged under Section 13 is trying to spark a debate of one kind or another.

The only viable conclusion: the CHRC was just making up their logic on the fly, as a pretext to let me go without a politically embarrassing fight.

That's a double standard. It's a violation of the rule of law: I shouldn't be above the law, and Reverend Boissoin shouldn't be beneath it. If he's guilty, I am too. If I'm free to publish his words, he should be too. That's why this case was the perfect lab experiment: All of the factors were "controlled" except one variable – the political power of the defendant.

I wrote back to the CHRC, pointing out their double standard and demanding (unsuccessfully, as it turns out) that I be put through the same gears that Reverend Boissoin was.

While I was at it, I also included a few choice thoughts on the CHRC's religious bias: "There is only one reason for [the discrepancy in treatment]: the CHRC is anti-Christian, and thus you excuse in me what you condemned in Rev. Boissoin . . . I note that the CHRC has never once prosecuted a "hate speech" complaint against any non-Christian, though there is plenty of non-Christian bigotry in Canada. No Muslim extremist, no Tamil extremist, no Sikh extremist has ever been prosecuted, though those communities are wracked with internecine hates between radical and moderate camps, that sometimes spill over into violence. But you'd rather pick on a seventy-something Catholic priest for publishing a newsletter. That's why you're letting me go – I'm not a weak, penniless Christian clergyman."

I wrote all this not because I'm a masochist; but because I know that I'm better able to fight back and raise hell than an impoverished preacher. I've got a Rolodex of talk radio hosts across the country; I've got the attention of politicians in several parties; and I've got a big, booming website where concerned Canadians – and friends of freedom around the world – have been willing to chip in for my legal defence fund.

In a way, I wish it had been me charged six years ago, instead of Reverend Boissoin. I wouldn't have gone so quietly; I wouldn't have turned the other cheek. Rob Wells's complaint was absurd. And I wish I'd been able to use it as a teaching tool, to show Canadians just what kind of creature HRCs had become.